Crazy True Tales - A funny book for adults

Anecdotes and hilarious true stories. For the coffee table, bathroom or as a conversation starter.

By Adam Douglas

Crazy True Tales

© Copyright 2019 - All rights reserved.

It is not legal to reproduce, duplicate, or transmit any part of this document in either electronic means or in printed format. Recording of this publication is strictly prohibited and any storage of this document is not allowed unless with written permission from the publisher except for the use of brief quotations in a book review.

Introduction

Laughter is the best medicine, but while the world's finest comics hand out joke after joke there's really no better source of amusement than real life.

The world is a genuinely funny place, filled with humorous people, animals, and things. You can go out in search of them yourself, and will probably encounter several in your everyday life, but it's always good to have an easy source of entertainment to tap into.

Crazy True Tales is a carefully curated collection of the funniest true-life stories Planet Earth has to offer. It allows you to get up close and personal with humanity's madness, mayhem, and mindlessness without putting yourself in harm's way. People have done some truly ridiculous and surprising things. One man's (often deserved) misfortune is another's entertainment, and there's absolutely no shame in that.

Our cornucopian selection of hysterical stories, anecdotes, and facts will have you roaring with laughter while also arming you with plenty of interesting icebreakers and talking points. Here you'll find tales of highly decorated zoo animals, hopeless business schemes, and criminals that got their comeuppance. These pages contain witty stories of wartime gaffs, rib-tickling political intrigue, and much else besides.

This book is meant for everyone. Keep it at home to entertain friends and family, gift it to a friend, or package it up for an eccentric long-lost uncle. It can provide light relief during long nights at work, knee-slapping distractions during the best of times, and cause enough to break into a smile during the worst of times.

Charlie Chaplin once said that a day without laughter is wasted. With this dossier of the world's most hilarious mishaps, misadventures, and muddles, you'll never have to worry about wasting a day again.

Burn The Witch - But Not The Cake!

The Salem Witch Trials are notorious around the world, and many people know about the 'sink or swim' test used to decide whether a suspect was in fact a magical miscreant. The other tests deployed by witch hunters don't enjoy quite the same notoriety, which is surprising given their total absurdity.

For one thing, some intrepid witch hunters concocted a plan to make 'witch cakes' as a means of testing whether a suspected sorceress was in fact evil. They took a sample of the so-called witch's urine and mixed it with rye-meal and ashes before baking the horrid mix into a cake. The foul dessert was then fed to a dog in the hope that it would fall under a spell and reveal the name of the guilty party.

Prior to the Salem Witch Trials, the slave Tituba helped bake a witch cake to identify the person responsible for mystifying young Betty Parris, but the brew didn't work for obvious reasons. In a bizarre turn of events, Tituba was then accused of being a witch herself on account of her folk remedy knowledge.

During the same trial period, a woman was accused of being a witch in place of her twin sister who had run off to another state with a lover. When she denied any involvement with the occult, locals claimed that she must have swapped bodies with her twin in the hope of escaping the trial.

Perhaps you could say they s-witched places.

Cat Combat: Taking the Fight to the Felines

What great issue has divided humanity for centuries?

Well, however unlikely it may seem, the answer just could be cats.

Felines were venerated and worshiped in ancient Egypt as the embodiment of goddess Bastet's spirit. In fact, the Egyptians respected cats so much that the invading Persians adorned their shields with them in 525 BC in the hope that the Egyptians would refuse to throw spears at them. They were right, and the Persians won the battle.

Things haven't always been so rosy for cats, however. In the 13th century, Pope Gregory IX declared an all out war on them. He believed that they carried the spirit of Satan himself, and it was his rhetoric that sparked the age-old belief that black cats bring bad luck.

An extermination campaign began, with thousands of cats being slaughtered between 1233 and 1234. Unfortunately for the Catholic church, this cull didn't bring about the end of heresy, but it did contribute to the plague which ravished Europe in the following years.

In killing the cats, the Pope had exterminated Europe's best line of defense against rats and other vermin.

Despite triggering a medical cat-astrophe Gregory IX also managed to blame the plague on Satan, who did pretty paw-ly out of the whole affair.

Prehistoric Man Slapped With Speeding Ticket

The much-beloved Flintstones are known for their prehistoric capers, and Fred's foot powered car is truly iconic. While the series itself is completely fictitious, many people have taken to dressing up as their favorite Flintstones characters over the years, and some have taken their efforts to the extreme.

One man in Gwinnett County, Georgie decided that he needed to make a real entrance while on his way to a costume party - and so took the doors off of his smart car before altering it to look exactly like the Flintstone's ancient automobile.

Cruising at speeds far greater than his feet could ever carry him, the man was pulled over by local law enforcement officers who were bemused at the prospect that he could in fact be powering the car under his own steam.

Having reached a cool 80 miles an hour in a 40 MPH zone, the would-be Mr Flintstone picked up a citation and was told to stop driving around in a doorless car with his dinosaur (dog).

Yabba Dabba Doo indeed!

Einstein's Most Unusual Misadventures

Who's the smartest man to have ever lived? While we don't have a definitive answer to the question, Albert Einstein is surely in the running.

Despite his great intelligence, Einstein got into his fair share of trouble over the years. Once while travelling on a train from Princeton, he reportedly lost his train ticket. As the conductor reached him, he searched all of his pockets and started rummaging through his briefcase.

The conductor recognized him and reassured him.

"Look, I know who you are, Dr. Einstein, and I'm sure you bought a ticket. Don't worry about it."

Einstein nodded and continued down the aisle before turning around to see the renowned physicist on his hands and knees searching under his chair.

Rushing back to him, the conductor said, "Dr. Einstein, Dr. Einstein, there's no need for your ticket, I know who you are and I'm certain you bought one."

Einstein glanced up from his position and said, "Young man, I too know who I am, but what I don't know is where I'm going - and that's why I need my ticket!"

Despite this mishap, Einstein was actually so smart that thieves stole his brain shortly after he passed away. Some 19th century oddballs used to covet the brains of geniuses, and tried to preserve them so as to carry out experiments that could determine the source of their intelligence.

Einstein himself had predicted this and expressly forbade any such work on his own brain, however the pathologist who examined him after his death decided to take another course.

On April 18 1955, Dr. Thomas Harvey removed Einstein's brain and took it home before dividing it up into 240 pieces. He stored these in two mason jars filled with celloidin, never gaining any real insight into the man's intelligence.

Harvey was tracked down to Wichita, Kansas in the late 1970s - and he was still none the wiser. Following a truly mad career, all he could muster was one unalienable fact: 'Albert Einstein' is an anagram for 'ten elite brains'. At least it seems fitting.

Coney Island's Sin Stealer

Roller coasters are just plain good fun, but they weren't really intended to be that way.

In the 1880s, America's first proper roller coaster was built by an American businessman by the name of LaMarcus Thompson. For a man who made his money in the hosiery business, he was very opposed to any pleasures of the flesh and was vehemently against hedonistic entertainment venues such as saloons, bars, and brothels.

Deciding that enough was enough, Thompson set out to make the world an altogether more pious place. He resolved to start with the most sinful place he knew - which just so happened to be Coney Island.

It was here he constructed a variety of gravity-based rides, and while he eventually moved onto creating genuinely entertaining attractions, his first efforts were designed to scare people back towards faith.

Thompson's first ride coupled a scenic view of the local landscape with the terror of plummeting to the ground in a rickety carriage without all that many safety features.

While his intention was to frighten riders, he actually made a fortune charging five cents a go. The locals loved it, and rather than becoming a puritanical figure, Thompson actually became the father of the modern rollercoaster.

He might have tried to scare the people sinless, but he really created the theme parks we know and love despite remaining incredibly devout and free from all that much personal pleasure.

You could say that his rollercoaster work was the real pinnacle of his career, and it was all downhill from there.

The Failed (and Dangerous) Soda Competition

There has been no shortage of amusing promotional competitions over the years, but one beats the competition by (air) miles. In 1999, Pepsi advertised a new points-based scheme in the US. The commercial featured a fresh-faced teenager flying a Harrier jump jet, while bright text promised that very same fighter jet to anyone who ran up 7 million 'Pepsi points'.

One entrepreneurial 21-year-old by the name of John Leonard realized that Pepsi points could be purchased for just 10 cents each, and inked a cheque for $700,008.50. Sadly for Leonard, Pepsi refused to honor his claim and even a court case couldn't compel them to part with $23 million dollars-worth of flying weaponry.

Following the near-miss, Pepsi updated the cost of the jet to 700 million Pepsi points and hoped that nobody could manage to drink so much of their cola.

Susp-fish-ios Behavior

In the UK, it's illegal to handle salmon in suspicious circumstances. It sounds like one of those arcane laws that dates back to the time of Shakespeare, but the Salmon Act only passed in 1986 and is still in force today.

Back in the eighties, salmon was seriously hot property. To avoid illegal fishing, the UK government outlawed suspicious activities with the fish and even extended the rule to cover others including trout and eels.

It's amazing how far some politicians will go to protect their supply of canapes.

His Heart Can't Tell You No

Rockstar Rod Stewart may have burned his way through two marriages already, but he's nailed the process along the way.

Before he got hitched for the third time in 2007, he revealed his plans for marital efficiency. "Instead of getting married again," said Stewart "I'm going to find a woman I don't like and just give her a house."

Getting Fruity For Nothing

In 2015, an Alaska Air Force base spent thousands of dollars on 'fruity' (in all senses of the word) lip balm that carried a message encouraging safe sex on its packaging. Over 400 were distributed by the base's pastoral coordinator as a free promotional item.

It wasn't long before an order went out telling the airmen to destroy the lip balms because they contained hemp oil - a substance that was banned by the US Air Force.

Not only did they make, distribute, and pay through the nose for a frankly ludicrous product, but they never even got to use it either.

The Great Emu War

Speak of war and you evoke images of the battlefield, with guns blazing, tanks thundering, and whistling missiles passing overhead. Cascading bullets and cries of anguish from wounded soldiers fill the air - but hairy landbound birds? Not so much.

Crazy True Tales

The Great Emu War was a heroic battle in which the Australian military took on thousands of the flightless birds. The hope was that this 1932 military exercise would prevent the emus from decimating crops while providing soldiers with target practice.

Perhaps predictably, chaos ensued. At one point, someone had the bright idea to mount a machine gun to a vehicle but the emus soon outran the makeshift tank and thwarted the military's efforts by splitting off into smaller groups.

In an embarrassing defeat for heavily-equipped soldiers, the emus largely managed to evade their attacks with guerilla-like tactics. They did leave in the end, but only because they'd run out of crops to eat.

Although we can see the funny side now, it's safe to say that the top brass were not emused.

The World's Most Unlikely Car Crash

There are plenty of (mostly) untouched parts of our planet that go for years without seeing so much as a passing traveler. One such place was the home of the Tree of Ténéré, which also happened to be the only tree for over 250 miles around.

This solitary acacia tree had survived the harsh conditions of the Sahara Desert for around 300 years. That was, however, until a lorry driver managed to crash into it in 1973.

The tree's toppled trunk has since been moved to the Niger National Museum, and it's to be hoped that nobody repeats the mistake of that HGV driver as a metal sculpture has been erected where the hardy acacia once stood.

Wartime Turkey Tetris

Animals have been used to transport cargo since time immemorial, but some crafty logistics experts have found more novel ways to use them than others.

One particularly strange approach to transporting supplies came about during the Spanish Civil War of 1936 to 1939. While trying to deliver supplies to a besieged monastery, Nationalist pilots strapped fragile packages to live wild turkeys in the hope that their flapping would gently lower supplies to the embattled monks.

Unfortunately, the story doesn't have a happy ending, as many of the turkeys flew straight past the monastery and carried the supplies far from their intended recipients.

As for those turkeys that did make it, the feathered heroes were 'rewarded' by becoming food for a hungry religious order. Now that's a tough gig!

Holy Smokes: The Pope Wars

The Catholic Church has long been a source of intrigue and curiosity, but some events from its history are nothing less than truly bizarre.

In what has since become known as the Great Western Schism, the late 13th Century saw three Popes try to exert their own brand of power over the church. How did this happen? Well, it was Avignon, France - not Rome - that played host to the seat of Papacy between 1309 and 1377.

Seven years after being elected to the Catholic Church's highest post in 1370, Pope Gregory XI decided that it was high time for the Papacy to return to Rome. Perhaps predictably, the French did not take kindly to this move and elected a Pope of their own, Clement VII.

As cardinals from both sides grew tired of infighting, they elected a third Pope - John XXIII - in the hope of uniting the church. To make matters even worse, neither of the previous Popes agreed to step down and all three excommunicated each other.

It took a further Council of Cardinals to elect Martin V to the Papacy and end the schism. If all of that weren't enough, the three warring senior clergymen were left with a very menacing name: the Antipopes!

The Japanese Tattoo Tragedy

Poorly-planned tattoos are a spring of universal embarrassment for those who get them, and a hilarious source of humor for the rest of us.

While there are plenty of gap year teenagers who've agreed to be inked after one too many drinks in a seedy bar, you'd probably expect celebrities to splash out for a quality job when getting their own permanent body artwork.

In celebration of her hit single '7 Rings', international pop songstress Ariana Grande asked for a wrist tattoo that spelled out the name of the song in Japanese.

Unfortunately, the request was lost in translation and rather than getting a neat homage to her latest musical feat, she got an enduring reminder of how to spell 'small barbecue grill' in Japanese.

It may not be what she wanted, but at least the singer can get her hands on supplies for a cookout whenever she visits Japan.

Moo-York, Moo-York?

While we're all used to hearing and speaking with different accents than others, it might come as a surprise to learn that cows also moo with a regional twang.

Studies show that when a farmer spends enough time around their herd, they start to pick up on his particular drawl. Although cows seem to have just a single word in their vocabulary, it's interesting to know that Brummie bovines from Birmingham might struggle to understand their cousins from Somerset or even from across the pond.

Bullocks to That

Most medical conditions require thorough investigation before doctors can commit to a diagnosis - but not boanthropy. In fact, the symptoms of this illness are so iconic that sufferers are just as likely to get a feature in their local newspaper as they are to get a prescription.

In broad strokes, boanthropy is a psychological disorder that causes sufferers to believe that they are a cow or an ox. They spend their time one all fours chewing grass, and may even let out a 'moo' from time to time.

If one of your friends or family members has started with the bovine behavior, they're in good company. The most famous boanthropy suffered was King Nebuchadnezzar, who apparently preferred hay to grass.

Whichever way you look at it, this udderly hilarious condition should be taken steer-iosly.

The World's Most Densely Populated Citrus Fruit

New York is widely known by another name - the Big Apple. Before it earned that moniker, however, it was briefly known as 'New Orange'.

In 1673, the Dutch captured New York from the English and renamed it New Orange as a homage to William III of Orange. The following year, the city's name was changed back following it's recapture by the British.

Nowadays the city takes its name from the prizes that were on offer at the horse races in the 1920s (known as 'big apples'). Even so, it's safe to say that the city was the Big Orange long before New York State even had orchards.

Where Hell Actually Freezes Over

"When hell freezes over" might be a go-to comment in arguments and bets, but you might want to be careful about using the phrase in future.

Situated in rural Norway, Hell is an attractive and hospitable little village - albeit one that struggles through extremely harsh winters.

While we can't speak for its biblical namesake, the Norwegian Hell contends with temperatures as low as -25 degrees Celsius (-13 degrees Fahrenheit) making it one of the world's coldest inhabited places.

Of course, such extreme temperatures also mean that hell really does freeze over.

Eat Your Greens (And Oranges)

Parents go to great lengths to get their children to eat vegetables, but can you imagine a government pulling the same stunt to get an entire country eating their greens (and oranges)?

During World War II, the British intelligence services spread a wildly successful rumor that Royal Air Force pilots had been eating barrels of carrots to enhance their night vision.

While carrots are high in vitamin A - a known eye health supplement - the truth is that the vegetable won't help you to spot any spitfires in the dark of night.

In actual fact, the UK's Royal Air Force (RAF) had been making use of their new radar systems to spot German planes, and didn't want to let onto the Germans. Instead, they spread stories of pilots bingeing on carrots to improve their night vision - and the same lie is told by frustrated parents to this day.

Long Time No Sea for the Flying Fish

You've probably heard the pop classic 'It's Raining Men', but you might not have heard the niche alternative - 'It's Raining Fish'.

While it's not actually a song, it is a reality for the residents of Yoro in Honduras. Once a year, the *Lluvia de Peces* (Rain of Fish) sees torrential rain batter the city. Once the rain subsides, tonnes and tonnes of living fish can be found littering the streets.

It's not exactly clear how the phenomenon happens, but some scientists believe that it may be down to water tornadoes that whip around the area and deposit whatever they've sucked up when they run out of steam.

Regardless of the real explanation, we can only hope that the citizens of Yoro like seafood.

The Real Journey to the Centre of the Earth

Conspiracy theories are often dismissed as farcical, but some manage to attract the attention of the powers that be.

In a turn of events that could have come straight from the pages of the classic book *Journey to the Center of the Earth*, a US military group received funding to burrow down to the Earth's core. Led by an army officer called John Cleves Symmes, the belief was that by trekking to the Arctic and drilling downwards, they would find a hidden society to trade with.

The expedition was approved by President John Quincy Adams, but Andrew Jackson took office before the team could set off - wiping out any hope of finding a long-lost civilization at the center of the earth.

Any Last Wishes?

There are plenty of wild, wonderful, and touching ways to commemorate a loved one -

but some people don't want to be laid to rest in the traditional way.

Edward "Steady Ed" Hendrick was one of those people. As the founder of frisbee golf, Steady Ed was a fun loving person who didn't want to go out without a, well, toss. His dying wish was to be molded into a frisbee and his family made good on that request. "When we die, we don't go to purgatory" Steady Ed allegedly said before his passing. ""We just land up on the roof and lay there."

It seems that Hendrick wasn't alone in having an unusual choice of resting place, either. Fred Bauer, the Procter & Gamble employee who created the stacking Pringles can, chose one of the signature tubes as his final resting place.

We can only hope that they didn't mix up the labels in the Pringles factory.

George's Uranus

The planet Uranus is widely regarded as a decent source of childish humor - but before it picked up its current name, it was called George!

When William Herschel discovered the planet in 1781, he named it Georgium Sidus ("the Georgian Planet") as a mark of honor and respect for King George III.

Despite Herschel's best attempts, the name didn't catch on outside of Britain and the planet was renamed Uranus after Ouranos, the Greek god of the sky.

Perhaps children would have an easier time remembering the planets if they'd left it at George.

A Marathon of Mistakes

The 1904 Summer Olympics was somewhat overshadowed by the Russo-Japanese war, but few participants would ever forget the men's marathon.

Fred Lorz may have been the first contestant to arrive at the finish line, but he had actually crashed out of the race after nine miles and thumbed a ride back to the stadium in a car. The car itself had then broken down at the 19th mile, and Lorz sneakily reentered the race just in time to jog across the finish line. Having celebrated as the winner, he then had his photograph taken with Alice Roosevelt - the then President's daughter. Just before the gold medal was awarded, his ruse was rumbled and he was then banned from athletics competitions for a year.

After Lorz's disqualification, Thomas Hicks was declared the winner of the marathon - but his path to victory was far from clear. Hicks had led the race by a mile and a half with ten miles left, but his trainers had to restrain him to prevent him from stopping to lay down. He was then given small doses of brandy mixed with strychnine - a common rat poison - in the hope that it would stimulate his nervous system. Hallucinating and barely able to stand (let alone run), Hicks was eventually carried over the line while he shuffled his feet as if he were still hitting the tarmac. He may have won, but he lost eight pounds during the race.

If the marathon weren't already eventful enough, it was also the first Olympic event in which black Africans had ever competed. Len Tau eventually finished in ninth, but his performance may have been hampered by the fact that he had been chased a mile off course by aggressive dogs.

The Great Potato Scam

Potatoes weren't exactly an immediate hit in France. That all changed when Antoine-Augstin Parmentier decided that it was time for change in the late 1700s, though.

Hoping to start a spud revolution, Parmentier placed guards around his potato patches during the day in the hope that locals would take notice and think that something valuable was stored there. By night he'd remove the guards so people would come to steal the potatoes.

While it's not clear just how many potatoes had to be stolen before they caught on, Parmentier has since been immortalized in starchy history - with a number of dishes being named in his honour.

Around the World in ... 169 Days?

Motorsport is entertaining enough as it is, but it's made all the more interesting by a healthy dose of misadventure and some extreme weather conditions.

One of the best examples from history comes from 1908, when the round-the-world race began in New York City. The route would take racers through San Francisco and onwards to Valdez Alaska. The planners then expected participants to cross the Bering Strait, career through Russia and Europe, and eventually cross the finish line in Paris.

Cars (and major roads for that matter) were relatively new at the time, but that wasn't the main issue. The Pacific Ocean was a pretty major obstacle for the racers to overcome, but organizers planned for everything - including them driving over the Bering Strait.

Despite meticulous planning, the race took a turn for the worst in fairly short order. While the first team reached San Francisco in 41 days, they realized that the route to Alaska didn't actually exist. The organizers stepped in to permit competitors to ship their vehicles to Valdez, but the race ran into yet another issue - the fact that the Bering Strait ice bridge melted around 20,000 years before!

It may sound like an episode of Wacky Races, but the competition did eventually finish with the winning team making it to Paris in 169 days.

Reality TV Takes On Politics

Television might often be scripted, but you never really know when it might cross the boundary into real life.

Volodymyr Zelensky was once the star of a popular Ukrainian television series called Servant of the People. He played the President of Ukraine in the show, following a plot which saw his character progress from being a school history teacher through to a public leader after his anti-corruption videos went viral.

Perhaps inspired by his time on the small screen, Zelensky then led a successful (and almost entirely digital) presidential campaign to unseat the incumbent President Petro Poroshenko.

Just a few months after his campaign began, Zelensky won and was elected President of Ukraine on a mandate of nearly 73%.

While there's no doubt that the President takes his role seriously, we can only imagine how good he'll be in the Servant of the People reboot after so long practicing his method acting.

The Medium-Rare Saint

Saint Lawrence the Martyr was appointed by Pope Sixtus II to help the poor and needy during the persecution of Emperor Valerian. Under the orders of the Prefect of Rome (who it seems was not a charitable fellow), Lawrence was condemned to death - and a painful one at that.

The saint was tied to the top of an iron grill and positioned over a fire that slowly roasted him alive. Not content with going out on someone else's terms, Lawrence waited quietly before exclaiming "Turn me over, I'm done on this side!".

Not wanting his captors to have a tough meal, his final words were "It's cooked enough now".

The Most Boring Day In History

The world is a busy place, and 24 hour news cycles have only made it busier.

Of course, the 20th century was no different - and along with two world wars there were countless scandals, skirmishes, and other surprises. That is except for one peaceful day, though.

11th April 1954 was still one for the history books, but only because nothing really happened. No notable births, deaths, or any truly significant events for that matter.

It seems that on one day in the 20th century, life really was easy like a Sunday morning.

Don't Order the Death By Chocolate

There have been plenty of bungled assassination plots over the years, with scores of 'ingenious' schemes derailed by poor execution and fate itself - but can you imagine trying to kill a world leader with an exploding bar of chocolate?

During World War II, German secret agents had planned to place some dangerously fine confectionery in Winston Churchill's War Cabinet dining room. They coated a small explosive device in a layer of rich dark chocolate and packaged it in luxurious-looking gold and black paper.

The plan counted on the 'chocolate' exploding after being unwrapped, leaving a trail of destruction (and presumably cocoa) in its wake. Fortunately, the plot was rumbled by British spies, who tipped off MI5 and sent out a memo accompanied by a poster-sized illustration of the abominable chocolate bar.

The plan may have failed, but it really does give a new meaning to the classic dessert 'death by chocolate'.

Russian Soft Drinks (5% ABV)

Most countries have laws to regulate the sale and consumption of alcohol - but Russia does things a little differently.

It was only in 2011 that the country classified beer (and any other beverage containing less than 10% abv) as alcohol. Until that time you could swill ale in the streets, guzzle lager at work, and freely give it to your kids as you might do with soda. Before that, beer had been thought of as a type of food!

Crazy True Tales

The new law may have changed things as far as advertising and sales restrictions go, but it doesn't change the fact that many Russians could drink any opponent under the table.

The Great Spaghetti Harvest

Did you know that pasta can grow on trees? No? Neither did most of the UK when the BBC broadcast exclusive images of Italy's spaghetti harvest in 1957.

At the time, very few people knew how pasta was produced and they lapped up footage of cheerful farm workers plucking strands of fresh spaghetti from blossoming trees.

Spaghetti, naturally, does not grow on trees but rather is made from wheat and water - but that didn't stop the BBC's spaghetti prank going down as one of the most iconic April Fool's jokes of all time.

The World's Strongest Magnifying Glass

You might want to think more carefully about where you park your car from now on, as a building in London has been literally melting vehicles.

The London skyscraper, nicknamed the 'Walkie Talkie' for its shape, is famed for its bending glass. The problem is that that very same glass used to reflect light from the sun into super powerful beams of light that would melt the cars parked on nearby streets.

In 2013, a nearby Jaguar sustained damage to its wing mirrors, badge, and panels - leading the local council to suspend nearby parking spaces to prevent anyone else from being caught by the ultra-strong sun rays.

The building has since earned a new moniker - the 'Walkie Scorchie', but that's not where its problems end. In more recent times, the hapless skyscraper has been blamed for increasing wind in the area, with the concave glass design causing gusts to whip between the pavement and its towering facade.

While remedial works have now been completed to stop the building from destroying anything else, its counterpart in Las Vegas has been busily melting the plastic cups and ice creams of passersby. It has allegedly even been warming up a local swimming pool - so perhaps the deathray isn't all bad!

The Great Cat Pajama Party

Crazy True Tales

What do international diplomats actually do? Well, some of them apparently organize cat pajama parties.

The US Embassy in Australia was forced to issue a lighthearted apology in 2017 when it accidentally sent out a burst of email invites to a "cat pajama-jam".

The invite came with an image of a cat wearing a costume reminiscent of Sesame Street's Cookie Monster, and the sender had an official State Department email address.

Supposedly the whole thing was just a training exercise gone wrong, but it's hard to imagine what kind of training involves an event with cats sporting nightwear.

As it happens, this wasn't the first time that the US endured a diplomatic incident involving cats. Among all the ill-fated schemes dreamed up by the CIA, Operation Acoustic Kitty is one of the more absurd.

In the 1960s the Central Intelligence Agency took to bugging cats with surveillance equipment in the hope that they would infiltrate Soviet meetings and parties to obtain critical information.

As you might expect, the experiment was a resounding failure. Veterinary surgeons operated on the cats to implant microphones, thin wires, and radio transmitters. They then trained them to wander around the area of the Kremlin and various Soviet embassies. Before the real work had even begun, one of the cats had no sooner been dropped off near a Soviet compound than it had sauntered into traffic, getting flattened by a taxi.

The whole project cost $20 million and picked up little more than the sound of cats lapping milk and chasing birds. It seems the felines picked their side before Operation Acoustic Kitty even had a chance.

Y2K's Real Victims

For a brief period in the 1990s, everyone seemed to think that the world would end because of the Y2K bug. Known more widely as the millennium bug, it was believed that software using just two digits to record years (rather than the full four) would result in power grids failing and the banking system collapsing.

While Americans stockpiled guns and the Brits began accumulating food and toilet paper in anticipation of the computer-induced apocalypse, little of consequence actually happened. Instead, a number of comical mishaps ensued.

In upstate New York, a video rental store tried to charge a customer over $90,000 after their systems showed that they were returning a movie more than 100 years late.

It was also a lucky (albeit short lived) break for prisoners in Venice and Naples, Italy. With a release date registered for 10th January 2000, the system flagged that the jailbirds had actually completed their sentences on 10th January 1900 - giving them sweet freedom a full week and a half before their time in the clink was up.

Of course, the real irony is in the name of Y2K itself. It was abbreviations that got us into the mess in the first place, so perhaps the millennium bug was a safer choice after all!

The Town Where Drink Driving is Rewarded

The authorities are normally concerned with stopping drivers from drinking too much - but one Pennsylvania police department turned that concept on its head.

The Kutztown sheriff posted a plea on social media for willing volunteers to present themselves at the police station. Their task? To get as drunk as possible.

The police department needed adults to simulate field sobriety tests so they could train their officers, and locals came forward in their droves to sign the waiver and get blind drunk for a good cause.

Some commenters even turned the idea of underage drinking on its head, by suggesting they might get a fake ID to enroll in the scheme. The police had set an age range of 25 to 40 years old for the trial, and it seems that people of all ages are happy to drink themselves into oblivion when there's a good reason to do so.

Taco Chance on Crime

In August 2017, a member of the kitchen staff at a Texas juvenile detention center signed for a strange delivery - 375 kg of beef fajitas. That might not sound too odd, but the facility never served beef fajitas, and there was no paper trail to explain why it would need such a gargantuan supply.

As it should happen, the prison's food services administrator had cooked up a scheme involving the beef. Since 2008, they'd been ordering the fajitas but diverting the delivery to a nearby restaurant - pocketing all the profits for themselves.

Six days later, the administrator was arrested and charged with a $1.2 million fraud. They were ultimately sentenced to 50 years in jail, and the case was all wrapped up.

Mic Drop At Your Peril

April Fools' pranks are harmless fun, right? Well, not so much if they result in your boss sacking you or even worse. That was the misfortune that befell some employees after Google's 2016 attempt to make the world laugh on April 1st.

Alongside all of the usual email options, the search engine giant added a 'mic drop' button to their Gmail accounts which, when clicked, sent a GIF to the recipients. So far, so funny, but the mic drop effect was true to its name and also completely disabled all replies to the message thread, literally shutting down the conversation.

While it's all fun and games to send a slightly snarky email with good intentions, Google just so happened to position the mic drop button next to the send button. This led to countless cases of mistaken mic dropping, and horrified email users inadvertently dialed up their passive aggressive sides when contacting their friends, family, colleagues, and bosses.

Unfortunately, at least one individual was fired as a result of Google's prank - and we can only imagine that the designer of the mic drop button faced the same fate.

Crazy True Tales

The World's Worst Supercomputer Chef

Artificial intelligence taking over the world is the stuff of science fiction, but some people take the threat far more seriously. Fortunately for them, the robots have got a long way to go before they can start their quest for world domination.

There are many stories that showcase our imperfect attempts at creating useful artificial intelligence, but some really take the ... Beothurtreed Tuna Pie?

Janelle Shane, an optics research scientist, set out to discover if artificial intelligence could design a restaurant menu that tasted less, well, artificial. She started by feeding over 30,000 cookbook recipes into a computer, and then programmed it to create its own dishes.

The result may not have been artificial, but it certainly wasn't appetizing. One of the robot's signature dishes was Beothurtreed Tuna Pie, with a recipe so simple that anyone could make it:

"Take 1 hard cooked apple mayonnaise and 5 cup lumps, thinly sliced. Surround with one and half dozen heavy water by high, and drain and cut in quarter inches remaining skillet."

If that doesn't take your fancy (and let's face it, it's not going to win any culinary awards) then why not try the machine's go-to kitchen staple - "Tart Cover Shrimp Butter Wol". This one requires a can of fried pale fruit to cover the drain, so at least the machine was aware of where the dish would swiftly be going!

Jolene, Jolene, Jolene, Jo-Leeeen - I'm Begging You Please Give Me This Prize

Forget 9 to 5, Dolly Parton was left working overtime to boost her image after losing in a lookalike competition to an impersonator.

While in Los Angeles, Dolly decided to throw her hat into the ring of a celebrity impersonator content without giving the game away about her own identity. In an attempt to blend in with the other Chers and Dolly Partons, the real country singer did herself up in big makeup, big hair, and an over-the-top outfit.

After strutting her stuff on the catwalk, Dolly was astounded to learn that she'd been bested - by a drag queen dressed as her!

Thankfully for Dolly's pride, she was far from the first celebrity to lose out in a lookalike contest. The late, great Charlie Chaplin also happened upon a contest while strolling around San Francisco and felt that he had a clear edge over the competition - given that he was in fact the real Charlie Chaplin.

When it came to the crunch, the comic failed to even make it past the preliminary stages of the competition. In his frustration, he even considered teaching the other competitors to do the iconic Chaplin walk - but no doubt somebody would have said he was doing that wrong, too.

Alexa? Wake Up The Neighbors

So-called smart assistants have embedded themselves into modern life. You can scarcely go anywhere without Siri offering you weather updates or Alexa suggesting local restaurants - but sometimes these assistants aren't smart at all.

For one tech enthusiast, Amazon's Alexa assistant turned out to be of more hindrance than help. Home alone in Hamburg one night, the smart speaker decided to take matters into its own... speakers? At 1:50am, Alexa started blaring out music at excessively high volumes. The music was so loud and persistent that neighbors were forced to call the police, but when they arrived nobody was there to answer the door. They had stumbled across a party for one, and only Alexa was invited.

Not content to leave the neighborhood suffering under the rule of a music-loving smart device, the police broke down the door and pulled the plug - leaving a new lock to secure the absent owner's property.

When he returned home, he was forced to head to the police station to pick up his new keys and pay the sizable locksmith's bill. He has since parted ways with his Alexa, and for that his neighbors are grateful.

A Most Expensive Unwanted Gift

Today Stonehenge is one of England's most important monuments, and is widely regarded as one of the great wonders of the world. It hasn't always been that way though, and over the years it has even served its time as an unwanted gift.

On 21 September 1915, a barrister by the name of Cecil Chubb purchased Stonehenge for the impressive sum of £6,600. Well, it might not sound impressive, but the same price tag in 2021 would set you back nearly £700,000.

Chubb bought the rocky wonder "on a whim" at an auction in nearby Salisbury, and brought it (or rather the deed for the site) back to his wife Mary.

Unfortunately, the grand gesture went unappreciated, as Mary had desperately wanted for Chubb to return from the auction with a new set of curtains. Refusing the gift, she then set out to the haberdashers to buy a set of her own - leaving Chubb with a pile of (very impressive and mysterious) stones in the middle of rural Wiltshire.

Keeping on the Straight and Sparrow

China has a deeply interesting history that spans centuries and covers everything from the formation of the terracotta army to the Great Cultural Revolution of the 1960s.

While the Asian powerhouse has achieved a great many things in its time, it's also had its fair share of blunders. One monumental error of judgement fell during the Great Leap Forward between 1958 to 1962. Chairman Mao Zedong had devised a cunning plan to rid the country of pestilence and disease by killing rats, flies, mosquitoes - and sparrows.

The so-called 'Four Pests' campaign made perfect sense to Mao, since the mosquitoes caused malaria, the rodents plague, the flies a nuisance, and the sparrows ate all the rice - well, except for the small matter that sparrows don't eat rice.

In their frustration at poor harvests, the Chinese government labelled sparrows "public animals of capitalism" and encouraged the public to kill them. Nests were destroyed, eggs were cracked, and chicks were killed by the thousand. Millions of Chinese workers also found new jobs banging pots and pans to scare the sparrows and prevent them from nesting in their local area, since it was expected that they would eventually drop dead from exhaustion.

The catch, as we've already explained, was that the sparrows didn't actually eat all that much rice, and actually consumed a large number of insects. Those very same insects were some of the most prolific pests any paddy farmer would ever have to contend with.

With no sparrows to eat them up, locust populations boomed and tore through the Chinese countryside - eating up all the remaining rice (and everything else) in their wake. As this was happening, the Chinese agricultural sector was left with practically no workers as they were all so busy banging pots and pans.

Eventually, the Chinese government was left with no option but to import 250,000 sparrows from the Soviet Union - and change the focus of their 'Four Pests' campaign to tackle the tiny (but no doubt very scary) bed bugs.

World's Most Deadly: Lavatories That Kill

Forget sharks, road traffic accidents, and workplace injuries. One of America's greatest predators is the humble toilet. According to some estimates, as many as 40,000 Americans are injured by toilets every year.

It's widely known that Elvis Presley died while on (or around) the toilet, but there have been plenty of other commode-related tragedies over the years, too - including the death of Britain's King George II in similar circumstances. Toilets have also been the site of numerous assassination attempts, including Edmund II of England and the Japanese Warlord Uesugi Kenshin.

The frequency of these accidents makes sense when you consider that the average person spends an estimated three years on the toilet during their lifetime. It's such a pervasive part of life that the Roman's allegedly had a god of toilets - Crepitus (just one letter away from an altogether more accurate and amusing name).

A Pricey Way To Stub Your Toe

The gold rush was marked by the desperate searching for precious metals, but while some people were spending every waking moment panning for the shiny stuff, others were (un)lucky enough to have the stuff in their homes without ever knowing it.

In 1799, a young boy from North Carolina by the name of Conrad Reed found an unusual and bright yellow rock near his family's property at Little Meadow Creek. Carting the 17-pound stone home, the family then used it as a doorstop for three years.

It was Conrad's father who eventually gave in and took the rock to a jeweler in nearby Fayetteville to learn more about it. As it happened, the now scuffed and scraped rock was a huge gold nugget which in today's market would be worth more than $500,000.

The discovery led to renewed interest in the supposedly gold-flecked rivers of North Carolina, and the Reed family kicked themselves for struggling on for years when they had such a valuable asset right under their noses.

Still, the super-valuable gold nugget did make a good doorstop.

The Curious Case of the Plumstead Ghost

Britain's oldest buildings are united by an unusual common feature - the belief that they're haunted. While we'll reserve judgement on the true nature of the ghostly goings on at the nation's ruined castles and abbeys, there is one ghost that turned out to be more parody than paranormal.

Crazy True Tales

In October 1897, reports of ghostly activity started to flow in from the local residents of Plumstead - a hilly suburb of London. Many people had seen a spectre near St James's Church and school, and a timid schoolmaster had been scared out of his skin when the so-called 'Plumstead Ghost' grabbed him from behind and bellowed 'Boo-hah!', and an elderly couple received a similar treatment.

Another schoolmaster went for an evening stroll the very next evening, and was accosted by the spectral assailant, with the same 'Boo-hah!' as before. Sterner than his colleague, this teacher had brought a large and easy-to-anger Newfoundland dog with him - setting it on the ghost who yelped as the dog sank his fangs into its buttocks.

News that the ghost could in fact be a man got back to the local schoolboys, and they decided to play their own game with the ghoul. One evening a hundred-strong troop of the boys marched on the churchyard, pelting the ghost with stones but missing and instead damaging a priceless stained glass window. The ringleaders of the do-it-yourself ghost catchers were arrested, but the police let them go when their schoolmaster explained what had been going on.

Later that evening the Plumstead Ghost was spotted again in the garden of a local aristocrat, who sent for the police. When they finally caught up with the phantom, it emerged that his white garb had been torn by the dog, leaving his bruised buttocks on display.

The annoying apparition turned out to be nothing more than a local engineer gone mad, and the story ends with our not-so-scary antagonist being carted off to an asylum.

Liechtenstein's Final Military Mishap

Much like Switzerland, the European nation state of Liechtenstein does it's best to maintain political neutrality. Unlike the Swiss, however, Liechtenstein doesn't have its own army - and that's probably for the best.

Although it's widely believed that Liechtenstein sent a unit to fight alongside Austro-Hungarian allies in World War I, that simply isn't true. It's army of just 80 was in fact disbanded in 1866 after, well, a mishap.

During the Austro-Prussian war, Liechtenstein's tiny army had been sent to guard the Brenner Pass between Austria and Italy. Bored through lack of fighting, they started to drink wine and beer, smoke pipes, and generally take it easier than any active military unit ever should.

After a thoroughly uneventful campaign, Liechtenstein's finest marched back to their capital city of Vaduz - but it emerged after roll call that there were now 81 men. As it happens, the unit had encountered forces from Italy, made fast friends, and brought one of them back to Liechtenstein.

Rather than celebrate the addition of another much-needed fighter, the top brass disbanded the army - who were clearly better socialites than warmongers.

Extreme Gardening - US Army Rules

Ever heard of extreme gardening? No, not the kind that involves speed lawn mowing or precision planting, but the kind that could lead to a full-blown war if you get it wrong.

It sounds extreme, but it's exactly what happened in the demilitarized zone between North and South Korea during August 1976.

The landscaping job was kicked off by the savage murder of two US officers who were trying to cut down a tree in the DMZ. Furious with the North Koreans, the US resolved to respond with a monumental show of force, and deployed hundreds of men, a handful of helicopters, B52 bombers, and an entire aircraft carrier task force. Their task wasn't to gain retribution for their dead comrades, but rather to cut back the poplar that had started the whole debacle.

The show of strength, known as Operation Paul Bunyan (named after a giant lumberjack from US folklore), saw the hundreds-strong task force go to war on the poplar where the officers had met their demise just days earlier.

It's safe to say that the tree lost.

Don't Kick The Bucket

They say that you should only go to war for things that you truly believe in. While we'll never quite know what the 11th century Armies of Bologna believed, their escapades do give a whole new meaning to 'petty warfare'.

In 1325, the forces of Modena are rumored to have stolen something of great value from Bologna, sparking all out war that resulted in over 2,000 casualties, the destruction of property, the pillaging of villages, and a landmark battle at Zappolino.

The priceless relic that led to all that bloodshed? A wooden bucket. To make matters worse, the Bolognese never got it back either!

A Bunch of Hot Air

Crazy True Tales

The damaging effects of tobacco are now well documented, but that wasn't always the case.

In fact, doctors used to recommend the stuff as a health aid and it was lauded as a cure for a plethora of ailments. As it happens, the use of tobacco as a medicine also doubles as the rather crude origin story for the phrase "blowing smoke up my ass".

Nowadays the phrase is used to suggest that somebody is insincerely complimenting you or telling you exactly what you want to hear. It's often directed at yes-men and suck-ups, but it had a far more intrusive meaning in the 1700s.

Back then, a doctor might quite literally 'blow smoke up your ass' as part of a treatment plan. That's not where the absurdity ends, though, as the old tobacco-posterior-smoke treatment was most commonly used as a way to revive drawing victims.

Although blowing smoke into any orifice is practically useless from a medical point of view, the belief was widely held. In fact, the River Thames was dotted with medical kits designed for blowing smoke up a drowned person's backside and the equipment was probably about as popular as the modern day defibrillator.

Thankfully the doctors eventually saw the error of their ways, but not after many years spent wasting their time filling the bottoms of long-gone drowning victims with smoke.

Never Work With Children or Animals

Doves are quite literally an international symbol of peace, so it's a little surprising that they aren't allowed to feature in Olympic opening ceremonies. The rule may seem unfounded, but there's a good reason why these docile birds are banned from inclusion in the pageantry of the games.

Back in 1988 it was South Korea's turn to host the world's greatest sporting spectacle, and people flocked in their droves to see the opening ceremony in Seoul. With tens of millions of people watching, doves were released over the stadium - but true to their character as wild birds, they just didn't want to play ball.

While some doves circled the Olympic stadium to the delight of the crowds, others perched themselves within the Olympic cauldron. Not wanting to fall behind, the South Korean hospitality teams lit the cauldrons in the hope that the birds would simply fly away from the fire. They didn't.

Crazy True Tales

At last count, 11 doves were roasted in the 1988 Olympic opening ceremony, and they've never been allowed since.

Suffice to say that dove roasting is unlikely to make it onto the sporting program any time soon.

Bonaparte's Bunny Bonanza

The history books will tell you that Napoleon's most crushing defeat came at Waterloo, but it may well have been eight years earlier when he was attacked by a pillaging horde or rabbits.

In July 1807, just after Napoleon had signed the Treaties of Tilsit to end the war with Imperial Russia, the emperor proposed a celebratory rabbit hunt. Chief of Staff Alexandre Berthier was tasked with organizing the merriment, and he went about arranging a grand luncheon. Berthier also gathered hundreds of rabbits and kept them caged along the fringes of a nearby grassy field.

The plan, of course, was for the furry fiends to be released and for Napoleon's men to chase and hunt them. As you may expect, events didn't quite unfold as expected.

When the rabbits were released, they didn't run away or even try to burrow downwards. Instead, they hopped, skipped, and jumped towards the world's most powerful man faster than he had stormed the Bastille. In fact, their swarming tactics got them up close and personal with Napoleon, and they even started to climb his jacket.

Unable to stem the constant flow of fluffy bunnies, Napoleon retreated to his carriage. Undeterred, the rabbits kept coming, flanking both sides of the cart until Europe's conqueror had the good sense to flee.

Unpacking the defeat afterwards, it was found that Berthier was at fault. Rather than trapping wild hares, he had purchased tame rabbits from local farmers. They didn't see Napoleon as a dangerous hunter, and were quite content to nibble on his bicorne hat as if it were a leafy head of lettuce.

Mr President's Rabbid Rabbit

Napoleon isn't the only world leader to have faced the wrath of the rabbits. In 1979, the then US president Jimmy Carter faced a similar dilemma when he ventured out for a solo fishing trip.

While casting his line off of a boat in a large swamp, an intrepid rabbit swam directly towards him and was only scared off when the Commander In Chief waved an oar at it.

The rabbit wasn't just amphibious, but also gigantic - leaving Jimmy Carter with an intriguing fishing trip story if nothing else.

Unfortunately, the escapade is also considered by some critics as the most memorable event of Carter's presidency - something we're sure he doesn't find bunny.

The Arrogant Architect

After successfully besieging the ancient city of Antioch in 540 CE, the Sasanian Emperor Khosrow built a brand new city that was almost identical to the former trade hub.

The houses were the same, the markets were the same, and yes, the toilets were the same too. Antioch's citizens were relocated and moved into their new identical homes, almost as if they were in a model village.

This might all seem like a strange thing for an invader to do, but it makes better sense when you understand Emperor Khosrow's motives - to embarrass his rivals.

You see, the new city was called 'Weh Antiok Khusrau' - which translates to "Khosrow Made This City Better Than Antioch".

Rivalries surely can't get much more petty than that...

The Real Story Behind the Sinking of the Bismarck

Warfare is never simple. From spies and espionage to turncoats and traitors, there's always something to complicate conflict - but that something isn't usually a cat.

During World War II, one furry feline started out as a mouse catcher aboard the infamous Nazi ship Bismarck. Several hours after that vessel was sunk by the British HMS Cossack in 1941, the cat was found floating on some debris and was adopted (or rather employed) into a new role as the mouse catcher for his former enemies.

Sometime later, the Cossack itself sank after being hit by a torpedo. 159 crew members sadly perished, but the cat survived and was dubbed "Unsinkable Sam" for his uncanny ability to survive shipwrecks.

The cat was once again called into action aboard the HMS Ark Royal, a British aircraft carrier. True to form, this too was torpedoed by a Nazi U-boat, and yet "Unsinkable Sam" managed to survive yet again.

He eventually retired to Belfast and survived until 1955 - a full 14 years after the sinking of the Bismarck. To confuse matters further, the cat was actually called Oscar - and you've got to wonder whether it was a good idea to bring a feline with such a bad track record onboard so many ships in the first place.

History's Most Lethal Medical Misadventures

Medical mishaps are a common occurrence, but few practitioners have been responsible for such devastation as Robert Liston who completed one operation with a 300% mortality rate.

The Victorian surgeon was renowned for being one of the fastest in the business. At the time that was a very good thing indeed, since anesthesia didn't properly exist and patients spent operations awake - a horrific endeavor no matter what you're having done.

The incident in question involved a leg amputation. Liston worked so fast that he accidentally cut two of his assistant's fingers off. The patient and the assistant later died from gangrene as the saw had been unclean.

The third fatality was a little more indirect. In those times, doctors and other spectators would watch surgeries from a gallery, almost as if it were a cinema feature film. During the amputation, Liston accidentally swiped a nearby doctor with a blade and cut into the fabric of his suit jacket.

The unfortunate doctor mistakenly thought he had been sliced clean open, went into shock, and died of the resultant heart attack

Liston may have set out to save one life, but he ended up taking three.

The Time When The Apocalypse Almost Happened

You've probably heard the phrase "saved by the bell". You might even have escaped a sticky scenario "by the skin of your teeth". But it's unlikely that you've ever avoided all-nuclear war by a hair's width.

During the Cuban Missile Crisis of 1962, Soviet Vice Admiral Visly Arkhipov was onboard a nuclear submarine off the coast of Cuba. His crew couldn't pick up any radio signals, and were unsure whether or not war had broken out. A decision had to be made between launching the sub's deadly arsenal and waiting for further instruction. Ultimately, the vessel's three officers resolved to vote and act only on a unanimous outcome. On that occasion it was Arkhipov's lone 'no' vote that saved the world.

Not content with one close call, the USSR entrusted just a handful of bases with the detection of missiles during the Cold War. In 1983, the duty fell to lieutenant colonel Stanislav Yevgrafovich Petrov, who was confronted with an incoming missile alarm.

In truth, the alarm had been triggered by the sun reflecting from high-altitude clouds which confused the Soviet missile detection system. It triggered an alert that suggested five US missiles were on their way.

Fortunately, the astute Petrov reasoned that the US would likely initiate a nuclear war with more than five missiles and registered the incident as a false alarm - all against his strict orders.

On more than one occasion, the US and the USSR have been saved from mutually assured destruction by just one person - proving that we never really are that far away from Armageddon.

Why the West Wasn't Really That Wild

The Great American Wild West has been the subject of countless movies, books, and legends - but it turns out that it could simply be one of the world's grandest tall tales.

The Nevada town of Palisade was actually a strikingly peaceful place. It had such low crime rates that it didn't have an official sheriff, and there were certainly no gunfights at dawn.

Things changed when the Transcontinental Railroad came to town in 1869, however. The conductor often told passengers that these towns were quiet and warned them not to expect the debauchery and outlaw behavior that was so commonly portrayed in Western dime novels.

Not content with being a disappointment, the townspeople of Palisade set out to improve (or rather degrade) their relaxed reputation by staging gunfights, bank robberies, and all manner of bloody bar brawls.

The deception was truly a team sport, as even the US Cavalry and a local Native American tribe got in on the action. The passing travelers were so taken in by the displays in Palisade that news of the town and its criminality spread like wildfire. Whenever the train pulled in, the locals got back into character, only to settle back into their relaxed daily lives once the tourists left.

It seems the west wasn't so wild after all.

Tax Jokes Anyone Can Depreciate

They say that death and taxes are life's only certainties, but taxation isn't always just on income. Over the years there have been plenty of unusual levies charged on everything from cooking oil to beards.

During the 1st Century AD, Roman emperor Vaspassian introduced a tax on urine. Thankfully it was the buyers who paid, but it brings a whole new meaning to "spending a penny". The urine from public lavatories was sold as an essential ingredient for use in chemical processes including tanning and to launderers who needed the ammonia to clean and whiten togas. The tax lasted for decades, and it really flew in the face of the Latin phrase Pecunia non olet - or "money doesn't stink" - because in this case it really did!

In 1705, the Russian Emperor Peter the Great started taxing beards in the hope it would encourage men to adopt the clean-shaven styles of Western Europe. It didn't really work, although some men did take to keeping coins in their beards to pay the taxman whenever he came knocking.

In modern day New York, there is a special tax levied against prepared foods. Of course, there's also a tax on food items anyway, and so sliced bagels are taxed once as food, and again as prepared food.

If these taxes weren't odd enough, Tennessee passed a new law in 2005 that required drug dealers to anonymously pay taxes on the profits generated from selling illegal substances.

Naturally it was a resounding failure, and drug dealers everywhere can breathe a sigh of relief at not having to file a return for yet another year.

The Dead Monarch and All His Doubles

Mistaken identity is one thing, but how do you work out who's who when there are 100 imposters claiming to be the same person?

After the bloodbath of the French Revolution, the then eight-year-old Louis XVII was imprisoned in the Paris Square du Temple, never to be seen again. His parents had been executed in 1793, and he had no hopes of ever reclaiming his royal title. He died alone and no doubt afraid in 1795, having suffered with Tuberculous.

Sometime later, scores of men came forward claiming to be Louis XVII in the hope of being anointed King during the Bourbon restoration.

In one case, a 50-year-old German clockmaker by the name of Karl Wilhelm Naundorff claimed that he was in fact the heir to the French throne despite the fact that he barely spoke any French. He spun a wild web of tales that suggested the imprisoned Louis had been first substituted with a wooden figure and then a deaf mute, all before being smuggled out of Paris in a coffin (albeit very much alive).

He went on to develop an early prototype of the grenade, and a rifle used by the Dutch military. He was not, however, the French prince. With the advent of DNA testing, it emerged that Louis XVII did in fact die during 1795 - proving once and for all that all of the claimants to the throne were truly imposters.

The Smallest Biker Gang in All of America

Chihuahuas are the cleverest dogs in the world - sort of.

The pocket-sized pooches actually have the largest brain-to-body ratio, and while there isn't necessarily a correlation between brain size and smarts, Chihuahuas are known to be exceptionally easy to train.

This might also explain how a rogue pack of Chihuahuas once terrorized a town in Arizona, proving that these tiny canines don't always use their powers for good.

In 2014, the residents of Maryvale, Arizona were besieged by four legged fighters. The locals made over 6,000 calls to the local animal control over the course of a few months - all to report a pack of pint-sized puppies chasing children.

The problem got so bad that animal controllers were forced to intervene - not with nets or tranquilizer guns, but with squeaky toys. Armed with a few dog chews and more squeaking rubber figurines than you could imagine, they rounded up what looked like a herd of Chihuahuas and relieved the townsfolk of their year-long struggle.

Luckily, not all of these tiny dogs are destined for evil. While other Chihuahuas masquerade as gang members, one perky pooch by the name of Gidget got a job as the face of Taco Bell. She even appeared in *Legally Blonde 2*, proving that some of these dogs do stay on the right side of the law.

The Elusive Pie-Making Bandit

Perhaps you've heard of Sweeney Todd, the Demon Barber of Fleet Street. The story goes that he gave up the bodies of his murder victims to the pie shop next door, but the inspiration for the fictional barber might have been just as gory.

The English town of Hertford is rich with history, but few stories are so strange as the murderous pie man.

During the 18th century, local sleuths noticed that many of the people being robbed had first visited a pub called the Maiden Head. Often an individual would have a drink and be on their way, only to find themselves beaten to the ground for their valuables.

One day, a man by the name of Robert Whittenbury was boasting about making £200 at market while sipping a pint of beer in the Maiden Head. On his way home, he was dragged to the ground and beaten. He suffered a broken skull, but was found along with the attackers who had tried to rob another man.

Once the dust had settled, it emerged that the local pie man had been frequenting the pub posing as a deaf drinker. He had listened in on the local's conversations, and enlisted his children to help him attack wealthy townsfolk.

Fortunately, his punishment was befitting of his crime. Before he was carted off for a lengthy prison stretch, he was shackled up in the town stocks and pelted with meat and fruit pies.

Suffice to say, the local police also had their p-eye on him when he got out!

Calamities of the Posterior Persuasion

The first recorded incident of 'mooning' came about in 80 AD, when a Roman soldier mooned a group of Jewish pilgrims gathering at a local temple. The sight of the soldier's posterior roused such a response from passersby that a riot broke out during which youths threw stones.

Responding to the fast-changing situation, the Romans called in reinforcement. Rather than calming matters down, the sight of further adversaries caused the pilgrims to panic and stampede through the streets causing the death of ten thousand travelers.

This wasn't the only time that bare buttocks have caused problems during a battle. During the 1346 Battle of Crécy, hundreds of Norman soldiers exposed their backsides to the English archers - thinking that this would frustrate and repel them.

Instead, the archers took aim and fired their arrows into what turned out to be a very fleshy set of targets.

Perhaps they ought just to have turned the other cheek...

The Florida Man All Stars

The 'Florida Man' has become synonymous with all manner of mishaps and misadventures - but some are far stranger than others.

One particularly hard of thinking Floridian decided to hand over a job application to a gas station near to where he lived, only to think better of his attempts to find lawful employment. He proceeded to rob the store in broad daylight, with the entire escapade being caught on camera. It's safe to say he didn't get the job.

Another man clearly not cut out for a life of crime was Danny Limongelli, who broke into an oyster bar and proceeded to take $150 of single dollar bills from a decorative wall. He tried to use his ill-gotten gains to buy a sandwich, but the cashier recognized that the bills were all marked with names of the oyster bar's patrons and Limongelli was swiftly arrested.

Another pair of Florida men spent two days locked in a janitor's closet at Daytona State college - only to realize that they could have simply turned the handle and walked out at any time.

It's hard to say what causes such drama down in the Sunshine State, but maybe it really is just the heat.

America's Love Affair with Midget Tossing

There are plenty of unusual laws in effect across the word, but few concern the sport of dwarf-tossing.

In 1989, members of an organization known as the Little People of America managed to convince Florida state legislators to make dwarf-tossing illegal. New York followed with a similar law soon after, but the rules were far from universally popular.

In 2001, a man who went by the name of "Dave the Dwarf" filed an exceedingly expensive lawsuit to overturn the 1989 law. The law meant any bar allowing a dwarf-tossing competition to take place on its premises would have its liquor license revoked. Suffice to say that Dave the Dwarf's attempts at reforming the law were unsuccessful, but that's not the end of the story.

In October 2011, a Republican member of the Florida House of Representatives introduced legislation to overturn the ban - suggesting that "the little people don't need the government to decide for them."

Attempts to repeal the dwarf-tossing ban were once again unsuccessful, yet similar pursuits remain perfectly legal.

For those fans of alternative sports, dwarf bowling involves placing a small person on a skateboard and using them as a bowling ball. Just make sure that your dwarf roster doesn't go on strike.

Spain's Laziest Person

A large company in Madrid once held an awards evening to raise money for charity. The event was something of a spectacle as the awards had been created for bizarre categories.

At one point, the M.C. enthusiastically announced that the next prize would go to the laziest person in the room. Partygoers were encouraged to raise their hand if they thought that they qualified, and most of the room dutifully put their arms in the air.

Ultimately, the prize went to a middle-aged man who seemed to show little interest at all - having not entered himself into the running by leaving his arms firmly on the table (with one clutching a beer).

The M.C. congratulated the man and welcomed him up to collect his prize, but the man was having none of it.

"Would you mind coming over here to give it to me?" he asked without missing a beat.

You really can't get much lazier than that!

Taking a Trip Down Memory Lane

In 2019, a man by the name of Elliot Curtis found an old Buchla Model 100 synthesizer in the depths of a dark closet in San Francisco Cal State University.

Wanting to introduce the old tech to his colleagues on the station, the Broadcast Operations manager of a media channel began to wipe it down when he started to feel odd. The bizarre feeling seemingly crept up on him after he removed one module to wipe off a crystalline residue. The substance had dissolved in his hand, and Curtis began to see the world from a different perspective.

Around 45 minutes later, Curtis noticed a strange tingling sensation. As it happens, the damp and dark closet had provided the perfect conditions for the lysergic acid to remain potent even 50 years after the synth had last been used.

Curtis had been tripping on decades-old LSD the whole time, and it's fair to say that the synthesizer was handled with gloves for the rest of the clean.

It seems the instrument really was destined to play acid house.

When Granny Fights Back

Age is just a number - at least that is what they'll tell you when you're recovering from a beatdown issued by a geriatric bodybuilder.

In 2018, a would-be burglar arrived on the doorstep of 82-year-old Willie Murphy. He claimed that he required medical assistance, and she readily welcomed him into her porch while she went back into the house to call for assistance.

As Murphy was dialing for help, the assailant tumbled through her door right into her house. All seemed to be going to plan for the robber, but it really wasn't his day.

Realizing that something was amiss, Murphy instinctively grabbed a nearby side table and swung it viciously at the man. In fact, she hit him so hard that the table broke into pieces - although that didn't stop her from attacking him with one of its spindly legs.

Not content with battering the burglar, Murphy doused his face with baby shampoo and went on to drag him through her house. Fortunately for him, the police arrived and it became clear that it was no longer the 82 year-old Murphy that needed assistance.

As it happens, the thief couldn't have chosen a worse house to target. Despite her age, Murphy was a bodybuilder who regularly lifted 225 pounds at the gym.

It seems unlikely that our hapless antagonist will be bragging about his criminal exploits any time soon - especially since they involve being beaten to a pulp by a granny!

The Return of Happy Slapping

Russia is a strange and wonderful land full with a diverse cultural heritage. That doesn't stop the Russian people from pursuing new pastimes, however, and in 2019 the country held its first-ever competitive slapping contest.

Participants were tasked with delivering the hardest slap, while also trying to lift the trophy for being able to endure the most slaps.

It was a last man standing affair, and whoever managed to hold out until the end would win.

Slapping between the competitors would usually end when one of the slappers refused or was unable to continue. The referee also applied his own discretion to determine if it was medically safe for a slapper to continue on in their fight for supremacy.

When all was said and done, a Russian athlete by the name of Vasiliy Kamotskiy was crowned the winner. The gigantic 370-pound slap-happy weapon even earned the name 'Dumpling' as homage to his size and the power of his attacks.

To win the championship, the Russian Dumpling had to face at least four other slappers - many of whom were just as big and strong as he was. Fortunately for Kamotskiy, he had a totally legal secret weapon - flour.

Before each fight he would coat his hands with the stuff as if he were in fact a dumpling. This meant that the blows he landed didn't sting as much, and he could keep on slapping to his heart's content.

Let's just say that you wouldn't want to have a petty argument with him.

Predicting the Vampire Apocalypse

There have been plenty of fun science experiments over the years, but Dominik Czernia's 'vampire apocalypse calculator' really takes the prize for the most obscure.

The physicist set out to create a digital tool that could accurately calculate the outcome of a real-life battle between vampires and humans. He created models based on different vampire stories including Bram Stoker's *Dracula* and even Staphanie Meyer's *Twilight*.

Taking characteristics from these works of fiction, Czernia created parameters that would determine how well humans could fend off the hoard. Some struggled with garlic and sunlight, while others were a little more resilient and really did need a stake through the heart.

In most cases, the outcome turned out by the calculator depends on the effectiveness of vampire hunters - but there are other issues at play, too. For one thing, it considers the possibility of a tragic shortage of holy water, while a few bad harvests could see garlic supplies plummet.

It all goes to show that the world is only a few rainy summers away from an all-out vampire apocalypse - we just needed a nuclear physicist to show us the way.

Crazy True Tales

The Animal Kingdom's Cartel

You've heard of guard dogs, but they aren't the only ferocious animals used to protect valuable assets. They also have far fewer teeth than their scaly compatriot - the humble guard alligator.

When police stormed a house in Coatesville, Pennsylvania, they expected to find drugs. They'd been scoping out the house for a few weeks, and had marked it down as a fairly run of the mill drug den.

On entry, they immediately discovered fentanyl, crack cocaine, and heroin. So far, so normal - at least for a drug raid.

What they didn't bank on, however, was the presence of a three-foot long alligator who they dubbed 'El Chompo' after the Mexican drug lord who goes by a similar name.

Notably, El Chompo isn't the only animal to have shared a name (and career path) with a drug baron. A similar situation arose in Kentucky when a 175 kilo black bear consumed over 40 kilos of pure cocaine.

The unlikely series of events was triggered when a former narcotics officer turned drug baron abandoned his aeroplane partway through a flight over the USA. The man had been flying a drug route from Columbia and had dropped off 40 plastic containers in the Chattahoochee National Forest.

Unfortunately for the drug baron, his plans didn't account for an emergency landing in a forest and his parachute became stuck in a tree. He eventually wriggled free from its bindings, but only to fall to his death.

When the police traced his movements back through the forest, they expected to find a cache of drugs worth $15 million. Instead they found a very dead (and presumably before that, very high) black bear.

The hairy junky has been passed around by various owners over the years, most recently having taken up a prime position in the North Lexington Fun Mall where he's known affectionately as 'Pablo EskoBear'.

Praise the Almighty Spaghetti Monster

In the mid-2000s, the Alaskan government set out to encourage diversity and educate people about the many different religions practiced across the USA. They enlisted the help of what they thought was a Rastafarian - but they mistakenly booked a Pasta-farian.

The local government of the Kenai Peninsula had arranged a sponsored prayer session, but they were more than a little surprised when a member of the Pastafarian clergy turned up with a colander positioned firmly atop his head.

The visit followed the decision of the Alaska Supreme Court to allow nontraditional faiths to participate in public prayer sessions. Although the local government had intended to introduce the somewhat more Caribbean faith of Rastafarianism to the locals, they had instead contacted the Church of the Flying Spaghetti Monster.

Starting out in 2005, the Church of the Flying Spaghetti Monster advocates for personal freedoms and mocks the connection between religion and the state. It's members worship (or at least claim to worship) an invisible drunken monster made of spaghetti and meatballs.

In his address to the crowd, Pastafarian pastor (or should that be pasta?) Barrett Fletcher called on the universe "to invoke the power of the true inebriated creator of the world, drunken tolerator of the all lesser and more recent gods, and maintainer of gravity here on Earth!".

While the audience weren't amused, he concluded his speech by wishing them all "an ample supply of their favorite beverage at the end of the evening's work" and rounded everything off with the final word: "R-Amen".

The Overemotional Sumo

What's the most bizarre festival in the world? Not sure? Well look no further than the Nakizumo Crying Baby Festival.

The celebration is held in Japan each year, and follows the belief that crying babies bring good health and fortune while warding off evil spirits. To make things even stranger, each wailing baby is paired with a gigantic sumo wrestler who must hold them as they cry.

Fortunately, no babies come to physical harm throughout the festival, as crowds simply chant "Naki! Naki!", or "Cry! Cry!" at them. Some people even choose to wear a mask bearing the likeness of the bird demon Tengu to incite the tears.

Interestingly, the entire affair is also a competition. The first baby to cry is actually the winner, while draws are settled by deciding who cried the loudest and hardest.

On one occasion, it wasn't even a baby that won - but rather his sumo wrestler handler. Seto Arisu was a 333-pound fellow, and yet he still harbored fears of demons and spirits. Upon seeing a priest wearing a bird demon mask, he began wailing uncontrollably and was awarded first prize.

Ever since that moment, Arisu has been known as the 'big baby' - and he no longer competes in the Nakizumo festival, since it's not really fair on the smaller contestants.

Caught Drunk In-Charge of a Horse

Coolio's song 'Gangta's Paradise' exposes the life of a gang member on the rough city streets. It was partially inspired by his time hitting the streets and getting mixed up in robbery and firearms offences.

The parody cover of the song 'Amish Paradise', was meant to be little more than a joke and was released by comedic artist Weird Al Yankovic. While he may have never intended for his song to become a reality, Yankovic may well have been blasting his hilarious cover in 2019, when two Amish men were arrested for being drunk in charge of a vehicle. That vehicle, of course, was a horse and cart.

Reports from the Trumbull County Sheriff's Department in Ohio saw two bearded gentlemen downing drinks from a 12-pack of Michelob Ultra and blasting bass-driven music from a stereo embedded in the back of their otherwise old-fashioned cart.

On seeing police lights, the two men jumped from the wagon and ran into the woods while the horse continued to trot in time to the beat. Nobody has come forward to collect the impounded horse to this day.

Surprisingly, this wasn't the first time that Amish cart drivers were chased down for driving under the influence. In 2012, four men from another Ohio community were arrested for drink driving and crashing their buggy into other buggies. When trying to escape arrest, one of them quickly tried to mount a horse to escape - but instead slid around in the saddle, hanging underneath his steed until the police could catch up.

If they couldn't get them for the drink driving, perhaps horsing around would have been a better charge.

Crazy True Tales

The Hunt for China's Strongest-Smelling Criminal

What would you do if you were on the run from the police? That's not a position most people will ever be in, but it's fairly obvious that you'd want to lay low.

Unfortunately for one Chinese fugitive, his attempts to avoid the long arm of the law failed due to his love of pungent tastes and hotpot.

In 2018, a criminal in the Chinese city of Nantong had scoped out a safehouse and was keeping himself to himself while the police scoured the local area looking for him.

Guo Bing was suspected of gang crimes, fraud, extortion and a whole host of other crimes when he took off from his home address while the local constabulary pounded on the front door. He eventually found himself living (at least temporarily) in a tower block which housed over 1,000 other people.

Bing probably would probably have managed to evade the law if he didn't have such a penchant for pungent tastes. As a former kitchen assistant, he had often watched the chefs at work and set about trying to copy their dishes as he was now living alone and needed to feed himself.

The hapless criminal was doing just fine until it came time to scrape garlic into the hotpot. Rather than going easy with a few cloves, he made the mistake of putting in 12 whole bulbs of the stuff - stinking out not just his hiding place but nearly the whole building.

The police came knocking to investigate the case of the mysterious garlic smell, and instead found a wanted criminal sitting waiting for his very strong dinner.

It just proves that following the recipe really is important, and that it only takes one cook to spoil the broth.

How Did He Fall for That?

Interactive art installations can be incredibly immersive, but they shouldn't actually put you in danger. Unfortunately, that's exactly what happened to a visitor to the Fundação de Serralves Museum of Contemporary Art in Porto, Portugal in 2018.

The famed artist Anish Kapoor had recently installed their *Descent Into Limbo* piece which featured a hole in the ground made to look like little more than a spot on the floor.

As he crossed into the room, the 60 year-old Italian man walked up to the art piece to see if it was actually a void or just a painting on the ground. To be fair to Kapoor, several signs had been placed nearby to caution visitors about getting too close - but the Italian visitor persisted thinking it was all part of the show.

Treading ever-closer to the hole, the art enthusiast fell eight feet to the bottom of the installation and was rushed off to hospital where he fortunately made a full recovery.

Before the ambulances got there, he did spend around an hour in a pit painted with the world's darkest material - *Vantablack*. He could see nothing, and had no concept of how long he was actually down there for.

We suppose you could say that he endured a descent into limbo after all.

Zoo Much of a Good Thing

Everyone wants to get their significant other a great gift from time to time, but some people take that to the extreme.

John Owen Casford is one over-enthusiastic gifter whose desire to please his girlfriend saw him break into a zoo under the cover of night. His intention was to steal a squirrel monkey, and he might have had better luck if he wasn't - by his own admission - "high as a kite" at the time.

Caford entered the zoo through an unlocked gate and broke two padlocks to get into the animal enclosures. He then tried to grab the monkeys, only to injure them while getting bitten in the process. They also slapped him brutally, and he was found with claw marks all over his body.

The sentencing hearing for Casford's crime is perhaps the most amusing part of the story, too. On dishing out a punishment for the would-be monkey thief, the judge addressed him and said "Only you and the squirrel monkeys know what happened in that enclosure, and I don't speak squirrel."

The criminal was jailed for some time, and his girlfriend had to go another year without a monkey.

A Most Unfortunate Interview

Some criminals are arrested at the scene of their crime. Others are tracked down by specialist teams. Some even give themselves up - but one criminal has to take the prize for the most stupid way to get caught.

Alberto Lopez was a former bank worker who had left his job in a flurry after being accused of stealing. Bank of America filed a theft report, and Lopez remained at large for over two years.

He was only caught after putting in a job application at the local police department - for the very team that was investigating his own crime. After he handed in his CV, the officers recognized that he was the man they were looking for, and played it cool by inviting him in for an interview.

When he arrived, Lopez realized that the interview was not the one he was expecting. The tape started rolling, and the police asked if he had stolen the $5,000 that had gone missing from the bank.

Naturally, Lopez didn't get the job. Instead he got some time inside for felony theft, alongside a lot of local news coverage that he's unlikely to ever live down.

How Cop's Caught the Biggest Creep in College

Creeps and criminals are hardly ever held in high esteem, but some really do occupy the toe-end of society.

In 1980, the officers at a police department in Southern California started to receive reports of a 'phantom toenail painter' from female university students. An unknown assailant had been sneaking around the campus library, painting their toenails and making off before they realized what was happening.

Police established a pattern of behavior, and dubbed the creep 'Leonardo da Toenail'.

It wasn't until months later that they apprehended a strange man after conducting a welfare visit on a property that emitted the strong smell of solvents. Upon inspection they found a man packing a bag and asked what was going on. He claimed that all was in order, but as they turned to leave he fumbled with his bag and out rolled 15 bottles of nail polish.

The police quickly connected the dots and served the man with a notice to attend court, but he was never seen again.

The toenail 'graffiti' continued for many years afterwards, and the authorities are still perplexed to this day.

He may have been Leonardo do Toenail, but the work of this weirdo is unlikely to appear in the Louvre anytime soon.

The Hall of Name

The world isn't short of places with funny names, but some places are more aware of their hilarious monikers than others.

The hamlet of Dull in Perthshire knows this all too well, and decided to embrace their drab name by pairing with the US town of Boring.

Crazy True Tales

In an arguably stranger move, the particularly grey English town of Swindon is twinned with Walt Disney World in Orlando. Nobody in their right mind would link Swindon with a fantastical theme park, but it does at least have a very confusing intersection that's known as the 'Magic Roundabout'.

Elsewhere in the UK, the Yorkshire towns of Once Brewed and Twice Brewed pay their respects to the beer-preferences of the soldiers who used to camp there. It's nice to think that the people there enjoy a relaxing beverage or two, but it's unlikely that they can best the residents of Rest and Be Thankful in Scotland.

With all of these unusual names, you might think it's best to just keep it simple. If so, why not visit the Devonshire village of Beer - so-called because, well, the locals really like the stuff.

The Belgian Exercise Regime for Couch Potatoes

The Belgians are known for their fantastic beer and chocolate, but they also created a truly spectacular exercise regimen that's just as effective as it is funny.

The instructions read as follows:

An exercise for people who are out of shape:

Start with a five-pound potato bag in each arm. Extend your arms outwards from your sides and hold them out for a minute. Then relax. After a few weeks, start using a ten-pound potato bag, and spin your arms in a circular movement until you can no longer continue.

Once you're comfortable with that exercise, move up to a 50-pound potato bag, and try to balance it on your shoulders while walking or running to the destination of your choice.

Finally, try to lift a 100-pound potato bag - eventually one in each hand - and hold your arms straight for one to two minutes.

Once you feel confident enough with all of that, put a potato in each bag and try again!

The Lucky Charm Catastrophe

President William McKinley was renowned for always wearing a red carnation. In fact, it was own personal good-luck charm and he was careful to never go out in public without one of the flowers tucked into the lapel of his suit jacket.

As a generous fellow, McKinley would always try to bring gifts for the people he visited, and would often give money and other valuable items away to the children in the crowds that invariably gathered wherever he went.

On greeting one crowd in 1901, he was surrounded by a school of children who naturally all wanted to take something from the President back home. He doled out sweets, coins, and even a necklace to the teacher - but he ran out of trinkets when the last little girl approached him.

Feeling bad, McKinley handed the girl his trademark red carnation with the words "I must give this flower to another little flower".

Sadly for the President, those words would be his last. Seconds after removing the lucky-charm from his lapel, he was shot dead by a man in the crowd.

It's impossible to say whether McKinley had actually been protected by a single carnation all those years - but it does seem like one hell of a coincidence.

The Perfect Crime

Heist stories are usually glamorous, and at the very least will normally have an ingenious twist that allows the thieves or the authorities to pull outwit one another. Even still, sometimes boring is best when it comes to crime.

One by-the-book heist crew took this to the extreme. Far from a high-speed boat chase, a breakout through the backstreets or even a helicopter ride from the roof of a target bank, the circumstances of their crime were almost comedic despite being prosaic and unsatisfying.

What was the crime, you might ask? Well, on May 2 1990, a 58-year-old man was working his usual shift as a broker's messenger in the City of London. He was transporting a bag of bills for a firm called Sheppards, and happened to be carrying deposit certificates worth a cool £292 million.

As he walked down a relatively quiet side street, he was held at knifepoint and taken for what was reported as the world's second most valuable robbery after the hold-up of the Central Bank of Iraq by one of Saddam Hussein's sons.

Unfortunately, that's really all there is to say about the mugging. The thieves just got really, unbelievably lucky and happened to have the IRA and New York Mafia connections to offload the spoils of their crime.

It just goes to show that the simplest route is usually the best one - whether you're tracking through the wilderness or trying to steal millions in broker's bonds!

When a Gesta-parrot Joined the Secret Police

During the height of the Cold War, a hapless Russian man made his way to the headquarters of the secret police. Of course, they weren't really that secret as everybody knew who they were and that they were always watching.

Upon arriving at the desk, he asked to see a senior officer. He refused to say why, and was left to wait for several hours before an official deigned to see him.

Welcoming him into an office, the Soviet official warned him that this better be worth his time and threatened to have him locked up if he made a false move.

Sheepishly, the man started recounting his tale of a lost parrot and asked the police-man-come-spy whether he'd seen a brightly coloured bird anywhere nearby.

Somewhat frustrated, the official reportedly started to threaten the man and demanded that he explain why he had come to a special branch rather than going directly to the ordinary police.

"That's simple" said the man. "My parrot can talk, and I wanted to tell you that I disagree with whatever he's got to say".

With that, the Russian man was arrested and his parrot never was found. Our best guess is that it took up a role as a public speaker somewhere out in Siberia, where the locals aren't quite so fond of the government.

The People Afraid of Words

There's actually a word for having a fear of long words - but perhaps you should actually turn the page if you're afflicted with this phobia.

Hippopotomonstrosesquippedaliophobia is - in all seriousness - the word used to describe a fear of long words. It has another almost equally inappropriate name, too: Sesquipedalophobia.

The phobia itself isn't recognised by psychologists, but we defy anyone asked to pronounce the name to do so without even a little trepidation.

As you might expect, Hippopotomonstrosesquippedaliophobia is not the only strange phobia out there. For one thing there's Deipnophobia - the fear of having to carry a conversation at the dinner table. Small talk really can be tedious, so it does almost make sense.

If you want to get really specific, there's also Arachibutyrophobia. That's the fear of peanut butter sticking to the roof of your mouth, and while it's not debilitating or life threatening, it's hard to blame anyone who wants to avoid that particularly unpleasant sensation.

Finally, there's Phobophobia which, almost unbelievably, is the word used to describe a fear of phobias. Now that's a phobia-inception if there ever was one!

How to Make Money from Thin Air

Modern art certainly divides opinion, but some of it really does push the boundaries.

In one case, a woman paid over $10,000 - only to receive quite literally nothing at all.

Purchasing from a gallery called the 'Museum of Non-Visible Art', the culture vulture swooped in to snap up a piece called "Fresh Air". In fairness to the art enthusiast, the description of the work was fairly compelling:

Crazy True Tales

"A unique piece, only this one is for sale. The air you are purchasing is like buying an endless tank of oxygen. No matter where you are, you always have the ability to take a breath of the most delicious, clean-smelling air that the earth can produce. Every breath you take gives you endless peace and health. This artwork is something to carry with you if you own it. Because wherever you are, you can imagine yourself getting the most beautiful taste of air that is from the mountain tops or fields or from the ocean side; it is an endless supply."

The problem was, of course, that the artwork didn't really exist. The Museum of Non-Visible Art deals in works that aren't actually real, selling descriptions of things that artists have imagined.

Surprisingly, this isn't the first time that somebody has managed to sell thin air. In 2003, one industrious Arizona man sold an air guitar on eBay. He described his apparent pride and joy as "an original Air Guitar from the 80s, used at a Bon Jovi concert in '89 for about 3 hours and only once since after six beers."

It seems like a fantastic waste of money, but then again perhaps we just don't understand modern art.

Crazy True Tales

Chinese Laws That Just Make Sense

Chinese culture is amazing, and hugely diverse. With such a massive population, it's fair to say that the country needs a pretty robust set of laws to keep everyone in check - but some of the rules are just plain weird.

One of the most bizarre laws forbids any man from eating another's wife... but only if he does so intentionally. There's really not very much clarification, but the law stipulates that you cannot eat a wedded woman as part of a meal. Whether you can eat a woman if she's not part of a meal remains to be seen.

An altogether more ancient law prohibits anyone from giving away the secret of silk-making. Anyone who does share the secrets of the process faces being tortured to death - so any avid silkmakers should probably keep their cards close to their chest.

There are also a whole host of words that are banned in China. Lots relate to military matters, but some are a little stranger. For example, you could be imprisoned for saying 'Winnie the Pooh' anywhere in mainland China, while ordering a 'Baozi' steamed bun will get you the same treatment. These are things that supposedly bear a likeness to

President Xi JinPing, so naturally nobody dares to say them.

If you ever wanted to complain about any of these rules and regulations, you haven't got much hope of that succeeding either - because the word for censorship is censored too!

The Bomb Recipe For the Best Ever Cupcakes

In 2011, Arabian members of the terrorist organization AL-Qaeda published a 67-page manual in English. The manual was called *Inspire*, and was intended to do exactly that for new recruits into their awful club. Rather than recruiting new terrorists, they just might have inspired a new generation of bakers instead!

Intelligence agencies in the US and UK already knew all about the launch of the magazine, and came up with a cunning plan to prevent any dangerous instructions from radicalizing anyone.

The authorities knew that the magazine was going to be released in digital format, and that it would be available for download to anyone with an internet connection. To foil this plan, the US Cyber Command tried to attack the publication's release by crippling its host site with a barrage of computer viruses.

Crazy True Tales

These plans were soon sidelined when the CIA realized that the magazine could be used to generate new intelligence leads, and so hacking was put on the back burner.

While the US three letter agencies were quarrelling, the British came up with their own plan, and a sweet one at that.

The new strategy started as the old one ended, with hacking. UK secret agents hacked the computers responsible for distributing the vile content, but rather than deleting it they decided to get creative.

First, they removed articles glorifying Osama bin Laden. They Also deleted stories that extolled the benefits of joining Al Qaeda.

Not content with destroying the spirit of the magazine, they also identified one article that gave instructions on bomb making. The article did mention the use of sugar for this purpose, but the agents had other ideas.

Rather than providing instructions for making weapons, they instead provided what was hailed as 'America's best cupcake recipe'. The new page looked exactly like the previous one, but now contained instructions for making mojito-flavored cupcakes and one delicious vanilla buttercream pudding.

The magazine's editors later found and fixed the changes, but presumably not until after some wannabe weapons makers had cooked up a batch of delicious cupcakes.

In this case, the terrorists really did get their just desserts!

The T-Shirt Weather Baggage Scam

Baggage charges are a real pain. That's an almost universally acknowledged truth.

The rules are always changing, and airlines set exorbitant rates for just a few extra kilos of luggage. Given the cost of bringing extra cargo with you when travelling, nobody could really blame Huang Jiao for his smart approach to circumventing the rules.

On arrival at Guangzhou Baiyun International Airport, the man saw a new list of luggage rates advertised at check-in. Not content with shelling out just to bring his clothes with him on his travels, he hatched a new plan.

On seeing the sign, Huang Jiao opened up his suitcase and started to dress himself with all of its contents. By the time he was finished, he was wearing 60 shirts, 9 pairs of jeans, arm warmers, and a pair of gloves.

Despite confused looks from the airport staff, the now somewhat larger Huang Jiao proceeded to board his flight for Nairobi, Kenya.

Problems arose for our hero when he crossed through the metal detectors on his way to the boarding gate. Sadly, he had forgotten that he'd need to be scanned and had left a few (harmless) metal items in his pockets - 9 pairs of jeans down.

He stripped those off, removed the offending items, and passed back through the scanners only to set them off once again. This time, he remembered that he'd forgotten to remove his spectacles from his shirt pocket - and you guessed it, the shirt was underneath around 59 others!

After completing the same routine, he passed onto his flight and presumably took up far more space than he'd paid for.

He was a man of principle if nothing else, but you have to wonder why he needed so many clothes for a week's holiday to Kenya!

Out of the Frying Pan, Into the ... Stomach?

Fishermen aren't usually thought of as ferocious hunters, and instead are usually happy to sit quietly in wait for their prey. Fish, on the other hand, can be down right vicious.

Crazy True Tales

One 28 year-old man was fishing on the south coast of England, and was about to pack up after a long and frankly unsuccessful day. Right before he was about to reel in his final line, he felt a bite and ended up landing a 6-inch Dover sole.

Delighted with his last minute catch, the man gestured for his friend to take a photograph. He took snaps from a variety of angles before encouraging his fishing partner to pose for some novelty shots.

It was at this moment that things took a sudden turn for the worst. The happy-go-lucky fishing enthusiast held his catch up to his mouth and pretended to plant a kiss onto its lips - only the Dover sole to take matters into its own fins.

As the man moved his lips towards the fish, it wriggled and jumped directly into his mouth, wriggling its way down his throat and into his chest. It took ambulance crews six attempts to resuscitate the man and extract the fish, which seemed happy to be thrown back into the water almost entirely unscathed.

You might have heard the saying "out of the frying pan and into the fire", but out of the sea and into the mouth seems to be missing a few steps.

Crazy True Tales

Drug Pusher Caught: Beard to Blame

Major criminals tend to keep a low profile, what with being wanted by the police for illegal acts and all. Some simply aren't that savvy, however, and there are few funnier stories than the demise of a dumb criminal.

One such bandit was Gal Vallerius, a Frenchman who had a deep dark secret: he lived a double life as a Dark Web narcotics dealer by the name of 'OxyMonster'. His site had become wildly popular in the US, and the authorities had been carefully building a case against him for some time.

The plan was to strike immediately should Vallerius ever set foot on American soil, and the drug baron really didn't disappoint.

You see, in addition to running an illicit web of narcotics trade routes, Vallerius also had a gargantuan and truly magnificent beard. It matched his naturally bright-red hair and so he really wasn't hard to miss in a crowd.

With such impressive facial hair, 'OxyMonster' couldn't resist entering himself into the World Beard and Moustache Championships in Austin, Texas. It was Vallerius' first time Stateside, and he registered his beard in the 30.1-45 cm category.

Unfortunately for the moustachioed criminal, his days of attending beard contests were over. He was met at the airport by some undercover cops who were less interested in his personal grooming habits and more concerned about all the illegal drugs he'd be smuggling around the world.

They hauled him off to the local jail, and onwards to court where he was read a list of charges longer than his beard.

Interestingly, rumors suggest that another of his drug dealing network had also been due to attend the beard contest but was taken down with an illness before travelling - thus escaping the clutches of the US authorities.

Now that's what you call a close shave!

Fishing for People

Things can quickly get weird in the great state of California. Even what ought to be a peaceful fishing trip to the pier can turn into a truly surreal adventure as proven by the story of an unnamed man who happened across an extremely surprising haul on one excursion during the hazy days of summer.

Having set out in the hope of landing a largemouth bass, or even a sea trout, the man instead was presumably quite disappointed when he hooked an altogether different local species - a very angry drunken local woman.

The woman, who was subsequently identified as 26 year old Daniella Hass, had apparently surfaced next to the man's lure and started shouting a host of obscenities at him before - in all truth - biting his line and swimming off with it.

The man's attempts to reel the young lady in failed dismally, and police turned up to coax her up onto the pier. She did eventually do as commanded, but only after flapping and flailing like a fish. Unsurprisingly she went on to face charges of disorderly intoxication and resisting arrest.

We can only guess at what creature the man landed next. While he'd set out for a largemouth bass, he was forced to make do with a loudmouth Hass.

A Pit-iful End

Overconsumption of anything is likely to make you quite seriously ill, but for most people the idea of an overdose conjures up images of hard narcotics and rusty needles.

Not for U.S. President Zachary Taylor, though. The Commander in Chief overdosed on cherries.

After serving just 16 months in office, Zachary Taylor passed away after eating far too many cherries and drinking too much milk at a Fourth of July party in 1850. The acidic cherries had combined with the milk to cause gastroenteritis. Hopefully his last meal was cherry good though.

Naturally the President isn't the only one to have died in particularly odd food-related circumstances.

The Swedish king Adolf Frederick reigned from 1751 to 1771 and was widely considered to be a good monarch who did much for his people. Rather than being remembered for passing the first legislation supporting freedom of the press, however, it's his death that went down in history.

On Shrove Tuesday 1771, the king observed the Christian holiday in the traditional manner - by feasting on many indulgent foods in preparation for Lent. Even today people tend to gorge themselves before forgoing certain foods in the run up to Easter, but on this occasion the king had grossly overcompensated.

Having already eaten breakfast, the king sat down to a meal that consisted of lobster, caviar, kippers, sauerkraut, boiled ham, roast chicken, turnips, potatoes, carrots, blackberries, sweetbreads, and duck.

This enormous feast would be enough to satiate most people, but not the hungry king.

After washing the meal down with far too much champagne, he decided to indulge further in semlas - a dessert bun piped with cream.

Tradition dictates that most Swedes eat four to five semlas between the New Year and Lent - but the King perhaps predictably opted for 14 of them. To top matters off, each was served to him in a bowl of hot milk with cinnamon and raisins.

Just hours later he died of digestive problems, and he never did get to start his diet.

The Santa Claus Paradox

Father Christmas. Santa Claus. Kris Kringle. Whatever you want to call the jolly man in red, there's no denying that he brings a degree of festive cheer to the holiday season.

Most adults are quite content in the knowledge that he doesn't *really* exist - but some scientists weren't happy to leave it at that.

Formerly known as 'The Human Neutrino', astronomer and astrophysicist Linda Harden made the empirical argument against Santa's existence:

Crazy True Tales

1. No presently known species of reindeer can fly. There are 300,000 species of living organisms yet to be discovered, and while most are bacteria and insects, it's not inconceivable that there are flying reindeer that only Santa has seen.

2. There are two billion children under the age of 18 in the world. Of course, Santa doesn't seem to handle the Hindu, Buddhist, Jewish, or Muslim children - leaving him with around 15% of the total child population (around 378 million). Using the average census rate of 2 children per household, that's 189 million homes to visit provided there is at least one good child in each.

3. Santa has 31 hours to complete his Christmas task list, thanks to the rotation of the earth and the various time zones he travels through. This can only work if he travels east to west, with about 822.6 visits per second. This leaves Santa with less than 1/1000th of a second per house to park, hope out of his sleigh, jump down the chimney, deposit the presents, devour whatever sweet treats have been left for him, get back up the chimney, feed his

favorite reindeer a carrot, and move onto the next house.

4. If 91.8 million stoops are evenly distributed around the globe (which simply isn't the case but helps with the numbers), he can expect to travel about .78 miles between homes. There just isn't any time for eating, drinking, resting, or doing what most of us must do at least once during a 31 hour period.

5. This means that his sleigh moves at more than 650 miles per second - which, for reference, is three times faster than the speed of sound. For comparison, the Ulysses space probe sailed along at a comparably slow 2.4 miles per second. Your standard reindeer will usually top out at 15 miles per hour.

6. The payload on Santa's sleigh introduces another complication. If each child receives nothing more than an average-sized lego set (weighing 2 pounds), the sleigh must carry 321,300 tons - not counting Santa who can be tactfully described as obese at best. Conventional reindeer can pull no more than 300 pounds,

and even if that figure was multiplied by ten due to their flying ability, Santa would still need more than eight or nine. In fact, we would need over 214,000 reindeer - a figure that dramatically increases carrot consumption times.

7. A vehicle of that weight travelling at such enormous speeds will create near immeasurable air resistance. This will heat the reindeer up leading to them each absorbing 14.3 quintillion joules of energy per second. In all likelihood, they will therefore burst into flames and create deafening sonic booms - deafening Santa and possibly starting a few wars.

Whatever you choose to believe, it's hard to argue with plain old scientific fact. If Santa has ever delivered presents on Christmas Eve, he's now dead!

Not the Knees

Thomas "Tommy Shots" Gioeli earned his nickname through his career as a ruthless mob boss.

He was particularly renowned for keeping his rivals (and even allies) in check, and kneecapped far too many men to count. In 2014 he was convicted of conspiring to kill three other mobsters and was slapped with a 20 year jail term.

You might think that was it for Gioeli, but clearly the criminal decided that he hadn't seen enough of the courthouse. He has since been named as the claimant in a lawsuit accusing the Brooklyn Metropolitan Detention Center of negligence following a 2013 incident on the inside.

The legal papers suggest that Gioeli was involved in a furious game of ping-pong with fellow inmates. During one particularly intense rally he slipped on the slick, damp floor. Somewhat ironically, he broke one of his kneecaps.

Gioeli claimed for 10 million dollars, but it seems his hopes of success are swimming with the fishes.

Dating Gone Wrong

Most people have endured an awkward first date, but they can't get much worse than the totally unromantic extravaganza that befell a UK student in 2017.

Crazy True Tales

Liam Smith had taken a (forever anonymous) young woman back to his home and she retired to the bathroom to freshen up. Unfortunately for her, she clogged the toilet in the process. Rather than leaving the blockage there, she attempted to save her later embarrassment by plucking it from the basin and throwing it out of the window wrapped in toilet paper.

Problems arose when she realized that there were two windows - and she'd only opened one, leaving a rather unpleasant package sitting in a narrow gap in the wall.

Worried that she'd be found out, the young lady confessed to Smith who agreed to help his date (who also happened to be an amateur gymnast) to pluck the poop from its resting spot.

Smith lowered her head-first into the small gap, and as you might expect she got stuck. After 15 minutes of trying to extract her, firefighters were forced to break the window.

The unfortunate romancer was left with no option but to start a crowdfunding page to replace his window, and it became clear soon after that the fledgling relationship was totally untenable.

Crazy True Tales

The Melancholic Robocop

The future of warfare, security, and even home help is most likely digital. The Knightscope K5 robot was designed to take up one of these future crime fighting spots, and was deployed to patrol the grounds of the Washington Harbor Complex.

Marking the event with the dramatic Facebook post proclaiming that there was "a new sheriff in town", the management of the facility really didn't expect what was to come next.

Anybody who has watched any futuristic sci-fi shows might recognize this as the backstory behind some form of brutal mishap involving the metallic crime fighter, but things didn't quite go in that direction.

Supposedly, after just three days of pondering its existence and the meaninglessness of robot life, the tin cop fell down a set of stairs and into a decorative fountain - where it died.

The future was filled with the promise of flying cars and other cool technology, when instead it seems we got suicidal robots. Knightscope did promise to replace the K5 - but hopefully this time without the "existential despair" chip.

Crazy True Tales

Murderous Crows

The town of East Vancouver in British Columbia should be a quiet and happy place - but for far too long it has been stalked by an unyielding and violent menace. A black, winged beast that terrorizes the citizens in broad daylight, striking fear into the heart of even the bravest locals, and carrying out hits on postal workers all whilst squawking and flapping.

It sounds like a demon, and maybe it is, but it's better known as Canuck the Crow.

In one area, Canuck managed to suspend mail services for longer than a month after attacking and injuring the mail carrier - who happened to be around 200 times the size of a crow.

The same bird (with a distinctive marking on its leg) has also been known to appear at crime scenes. In one case, the winged beast turned up after the police had shot a knife-wielding man, only to swoop down, steal the knife and fly off with it.

Canuck dropped the knife when the cop gave chase, but who knows what he had planned.

Not long afterwards, Canuck surfaced again at the local McDonald's where he is a regular thug. Customers were eventually able to corral the bird and toss him out of the restaurant, but it's only a matter of time before the winged miscreant returns.

With this bird, it's easy to see why they call a group of crows a Murder!

Bar Snacks on the Byway

Motoring accidents are never good news, but sometimes they have a happy and at the least amusing ending.

When emergency crews were called to the scene of a highway collision in 2016, they probably expected to see the worst. The stretch of road was known for high speed incidents, and they had often dealt with destruction, death, injuries, and even the shells of burned out cars.

This time, they were greeted by an altogether tastier sight. One of the vehicles had been carrying thousands of packets of Frito-Lay potato chips, while the other had been hauling crates upon crates of Busch beer.

The contents of the trucks had been deposited all over the world, in a scene that was reminiscent of the world's grandest Super Bowl party.

Both truck drivers walked away without so much as a scratch, and some thirsty locals even ventured out in search of beer and snacks.

On another occasion, road cleanup crews were dispatched to a turnpike in New Jersey. Two truckers had collided there, too - but this time the roadside meal was a little more substantial.

One had been carrying freshly baked bread, and had crashed into another packed to the brim with cured deli meats. If the emergency workers were switched on, they would have simply ordered 100 gallons of mayonnaise to the scene and cleaned up in style.

The Most Uncomfortable Sport Ever Played

Sport is meant to push your body to the limits, and see how well you can perform within the confines of an often high pressure game. American football, rugby, lacrosse, and wrestling can all be rough sports, but they don't even come close to the levels of discomfort experienced when playing one of the world's least conventional competitive games - flagpole sitting.

The sport was popular during the 1920s and 1930s, when Alvin 'Shipwreck' Kelly made a name for himself by sitting atop flag poles and other strange pointy places for extended periods.

Kelly was a strange character before his flagpole sitting stunts. For one thing, he claimed to have survived the shipwreck of the Titanic - a claim that was dismissed and proven to be false.

He may not have been truthful about his origins, but his nickname still stood. Rather than going down into the depths with a vessel, he gained the name 'shipwreck' from his career as a boxer - where critics often claimed he was "adrift and ready to sink" as early as round 1.

A colorful character, he went on to popularize flagpole sitting across the US - even staying perched on one pole in St Louis for seven days and one hour. Not content with that, he also managed a 49-day record in Atlantic City.

Whilst up there he had to live pretty normally, so would shave, eat, and brush his teeth while sitting on the pole. He learned to sleep sitting upright, pushing his thumbs into holes in the pole so he would wake up from the pain if he started leaning.

It's believed that he spent around 20,000 hours sitting on flagpoles, but despite his best efforts the sport was in its dying days. The Bronx police were tired of his antics and threatened to cut down his pole, arresting him following an inevitable descent.

You could say that Kelly had high standards, at least until he was banned from ascending flagpoles!

19th Century Online Dating

Online dating sites have made it quicker and easier to find potential matches than ever before. Things haven't always been so simple, though, and lonely hearts columns used to be far more prevalent than they are now.

In the 1800s, one young agricultural worker took to advertising in the local newspaper and set a high standard - with a good set of teeth and a hankering for a "person of the female persuasion".

His endearing ad read as follows:

"I am eighteen years old, have a good set of teeth, and believe in Andy Johnson, the star-spangled banner, and the 4th of July. I have taken up a State lot, cleared up eighteen acres last year, and seeded ten of it down. My buckwheat looks first-rate, and the oats and potatoes are bully. I have got nine sheep, a two-year-old bull, and two heifers, besides a house and barn. I want to get married. I want to buy bread-and-butter, hoop-skirts, and waterfalls for some person of the female persuasion during life."

The somewhat distraught and romance-ready young farmer signed off: "That's what's the matter with me. But I don't know how to do it."

Simpler times, same old problems.

The Safe That Killed Jack Daniels

Jack Daniels was a deeply interesting man. Having run away from home when he was just seven, he ended up in the whiskey business and established one of the most popular alcohol brands in the world.

Many decades after establishing his successful distillery, Jack came into work one morning and decided to get some paperwork done before everybody else arrived. He needed to get into the safe, but had trouble remembering the combination and so couldn't open its dead bolted door.

Frustrated, Jack kicked the safe with his left foot - causing an almighty pain to shoot up his leg. He had broken his toe, and left a nasty wound on it to boot.

Sadly for Jack, the wound gave him a nasty infection and his foot had to be amputated. Despite preventative efforts, the gangrene continued to circulate through his system and he eventually lost his left leg.

He died in 1911 due to complications arising from the infection, but the doctors were perplexed at his unfortunate circumstances. Had he only dipped the wounded toe in his own whiskey, he would never have contracted the infection in the first place.

The General Without a Leg to Stand On

The Mexican general Antonio Lopez de Santa Anna was always an interesting fellow. Despite being defeated by Texan revolutionaries, he was once again called up to defend his nation from the French who had sent troops to recover an unpaid debt from the Mexican government.

The French set up blockades around key Mexican forts, and sent a large force to capture Vera Cruz - General Santa Anna's main base of operations.

Infuriated, Santa Anna came out of retirement and scrambled to save the city. His leg was hit by French cannon fire during the ensuing battle, but he miraculously survived.

Sadly for Santa Anna, his leg was not so lucky. The limb was amputated, and the war ended when Mexico paid the money it owed to the French.

Some four years later, Santa Anna was struck with a very diva-like idea. He insisted that his leg be dug up and reburied with full military honors. The funeral incorporated cannon salutes, lengthy speeches, many reverent prayers, and delicate poetry recited in memory of the general's leg.

The (now most likely rotten) leg itself was then put into a crystal vase and buried beneath a gigantic and elaborate monument in the Santa Paula cemetery.

Santa Anna then used the following publicity to successfully run for the Mexican Presidency, only to lose his prosthetic leg during the 1847 Mexican-American war.

That false limb still remains in the Illinois State Military Museum, and isn't likely to be getting an elaborate funeral ceremony any time soon.

Surrender or Fry!

Hamilton Hume and William Hovell were a pair of Australian explorers who are perhaps best known for their amusing and almost always ridiculous exploits.

Their adventures saw them argue quite frequently, and at one point Hume had threatened to throw Hovell into the Murray River. Notably, Hovell told everyone that he would float out into the Western Port Bay which was in the other direction. His poor sense of direction was a defining characteristic, and presumably one that was very unhelpful for an explorer to possess.

Having survived the river incident, the two intrepid explorers managed to get themselves into another fight when Hume constantly made Hovell cross rivers. It would be unfair to assign blame solely to Hume, though, since Hovell did also lead them on plenty of aimless expeditions.

Their most famous quarrel came about while deciding how best to proceed over steep terrain. Hume thought that they should walk around a mountain, while Hovell wanted to dig through the narrowest passage of rock.

The explorers decided that the only way forward was to split up, and divided up their provisions. That's understandable, but the fact that they cut their tent in half makes little sense.

The real brawl started when it came time to divide up the expedition's frying pan, which was supposedly of great sentimental value to the oddballs.

They fought over it, each pulling in different directions until it fell into two pieces. One man took the pan, the other took the handle.

It's hard to know what the explorer with a pan handle did about cooking, but the other also had issues since neither partner had brought any gloves to contend with a searing hot metal pan with no handle.

The Great Lavatory Pilgrimage

People will go a long way for their religion, yet there are some supposedly holy sites that probably aren't worth venturing to.

When water started to trickle from a statue of Jesus Christ at a Mumbai catholic church, the locals quickly declared a miracle. They began collecting the holy water, and the Church of Our Lady of Velankanni became something of a pilgrimage hotspot for India's Christian community.

In an unlikely turn of events, the congregation were frustrated to learn that it was not in fact the tears of the Messiah that they'd been drinking. The arrival of Sanal Edamaruku saw the discharge identified not so much as holy water, but rather the result of holey plumbing.

Angry at his claims, the locals sought to exile him to Finland after a court case was lodged in an attempt to send him to jail for blasphemy.

Despite the congregation's fury at Edamaruku, his claims about the supposed literal tears of Jesus Christ turned out to be true. Behind the church stood a public latrine, and its drainage pipes had become clogged. This caused sewage water to leak through the statue's eyes in one of the world's most unfortunate plumbing incidents.

It's never easy to let go of your beliefs, but you probably should if they involve drinking toilet water.

How Hubris Killed Harry Houdini

For more than 30 years, the Hungarian Harry Houdini amazed audiences with his unusual stunts and seemingly superhuman skills. He jumped from bridges whilst wearing leg irons, slithered out of milk cans filled with water, and created an infamous "Chinese Water Torture Cell" where he was submerged and suspended upside down.

Crazy True Tales

His death defying getaways typically involved some form of trickery, but they were also genuinely risky. In 1915, for instance, Houdini almost died by suffocation while shackled and buried under six feet of soil.

Given that Houdini had survived so many close calls in the past, his death is somewhat surprising. In 1926, the performer entertained a packed house in Detroit but was then rushed to hospital with appendicitis. He died a week later leaving many fans thoroughly confused.

In actual fact, it's unlikely he'd ever had appendicitis at all. Weeks earlier, Houdini had shackled himself into his Chinese Water Torture Cell in new York. he was then struck on the leg by some faulty equipment, and limped throughout the remainder of his show.

He had actually sustained a fractured left ankle, but decided to continue his tour. Whilst moving around the US, he gave a guest lecture at McGill University and invited some of the students to visit him in the Princess Theatre. While there, one of the students asked if it was true that Houdini could resist almost any hard punch to his abdomen.

Houdini, not missing a beat, replied that he could and invited the student to try. With that, he delivered four to five incredibly forceful blows which caused the unprepared

Houdini (who had been reclining on a chair) in considerable pain.

Brushing off the incident, he went on to perform only to complain of discomfort and stomach cramps. It turned out that the punches had ruptured his appendix and poisoned his internal organs. He died shortly after attending the hospital.

Notably, many looked to Houdini himself to explain his death. He had promised his wife Bess that he would attempt to contact her from beyond the grave, and she held an annual seance for ten years before calling time on his final attempted student. #

In the end it was likely hubris that finished Houdini off, and he had been taking punches for several weeks before that fateful student stepped up to the plate.

Much like Houdini's other tricks, you could say that it was a stage he was going through.

The Murderer's Pen Pal

Society has a strange curiosity with the incarcerated. Whilst most people would agree that mass murderers should do their time (and plenty of it), a substantial core of individuals are so fascinated with high profile prisoners that they just can't resist striking up a relationship.

That wasn't the case with one of Australia's most notorious murderers, however. Instead, it was Ned Kelly who struck up the relationship by sending an incredibly unusual gift long before he even made it to jail.

One of his strangest exploits came when he came to the defense of his friend Ben Gould. Gould had been accused of stealing a horse, and Ned resolved to teach the accuser a lesson - by writing a strongly worded letter to the man's wife and sending it accompanied by a box of calves' testicles.

It's a rather unusual tactic, but one that we can only imagine works well as a form of psychological warfare.

Before he took to the bush, Ned also battered a policeman who had noticed him riding around on a stolen horse. To embarrass the lawman further, Ned then rode around on the man's back for several days before leaving him as a worn-out mess.

Horseplay is one thing, but that takes the calve's testicle!

A Novel Proposition

Relations between the US and China have always been a little rocky, but there have been periods when tensions have thawed.

During the 1970s, President Richard Nixon's security adviser Henry Kissinger enjoyed a particularly friendly relationship with China's Chairman Mao. Towards the end of the Cold War, Mao was chatting casually with Kissinger about potential trade arrangements when he offered a very strange shipping consignment.

What was this "novel proposition", as so eloquently put by Kissinger?

Well, Mao was willing to admit that China was a poor country. To combat overpopulation and famine, his plan was to give 10 million Chinese women to the United States.

It's not all that surprising that Kissinger declined the offer, but he did first have to take it to the President to comply with standard diplomatic procedures..

Nixon was once quoted as saying that "When the President does it, that means it's not illegal", so we wouldn't be that shocked if he'd decided to accept.

A Hay-nous Crime

Crazy True Tales

Crimes against fashion usually go unpunished, but the Straw Hat Riot goes to show that some trends just won't be tolerated.

During the early 20th century, any men who wore straw hats after 15 September could expect to be ridiculed. Their hats were frequently snatched from their heads and crushed - but there were times when mobs of teenage thugs would assault straw hat wearers in New York City.

Men did commonly wear hats during the Roaring Twenties, but societal norms dictated a strict calendar that all but banned straw boaters after 15 September.

It became so common for passersby to remove the straw hats of anyone caught wearing them after the cutoff that newspapers started to caution people of the impending date.

On more than one occasion, police had to intervene to protect "straw-lidded pedestrians" and a Pittsburgh Press article from September 1910 noted that it was socially acceptable for stockbrokers to destroy each other's hats as they were among friends.

This rule was still in effect twelve years later, but tensions had come to a head. On 13 September - a full two days before the ban came into effect - some young men started to get ahead of themselves and destroyed the hats of factory workers in Manhattan.

When the gang tried to pull the same stunt on a number of longshoremen, the men retaliated and a huge brawl broke out. The fight swelled and closed traffic on the Manhattan Bridge, continuing for several days.

Many young boys took to roaming the streets with large sticks, and some even had nails protruding from the ends to make it easier to hook the hats from people's heads. Most were too young to face proper punishment, and so were sentenced to a spanking instead.

A New York Tribune article from the time reported that: "Boys who were guided by the calendar rather than the weather, and most of all by their own trouble-making proclivities, indulged in a straw hat smashing orgy throughout the city last night. A dozen or more were arrested and seven were spanked ignominiously by their parents in the East 104th Street police station by order of the lieutenant at his desk."

Despite all the furore, the riot proved to be a boon for hat stores who stayed open late to cater for men who feared being attacked.

Crazy True Tales

By 1925, President Coolidge decided that enough was enough. He ended the fashion deadline, and (t)hat was (t)hat.

The Goldfish Derby

You've heard of the Kentucky Derby, and perhaps even the Epsom Derby, but they're well established and far from unusual. Quite apart from those horse racing events, I give to you - The Goldfish Derby!

In 1939, one enterprising Harvard freshman swallowed a live fish as a publicity stunt whilst running for class president. Lothrop Withington Jr. then prompted a goldfish-swallowing craze that spread among college campuses.

Mr Withington was apparently well-versed in the 'sport' of goldfish eating when he took on the dare, and chewed well before winning a bet. Unlike him, one Mr Frank Pope Jr. did not chew despite having doused his pet (snack) in salt and pepper. Although he choked a lot, it seemed that he had won the contest.

To regain the trophy for his alma mater, Harvard's Irving Clark Jr. polished off 24 goldfish, sucking down one after another. He did also offer to eat a bug for a nickel, an angleworm for a dime, and a beetle for a quarter. It will come as no shock to you that nobody wanted to take him up on those offers.

A few hours later, Gilbert Hollandersky from the University of Pennsylvania tried his hand at the sport. He guzzled 25 goldfish and cleansed his palette with a steak dinner. He was quickly outdone by the University of Michigan's Julius Aisner with 28 goldfish, Boston College's Donald V Mulcahy with 29 (and three bottles of milk), and Thereupon Albright College's Mike Bonner who managed 33 of the orange blighters.

Three policemen and 100 cheering students then watched the next champion, M.I.T's Albert E Hayes Jr., wash down some 42 fish with four bottles of soda. He only stopped because 42 was his class number, but was rapidly outcompeted by Clark University's Joseph Deliberato.

Following this bout of competitive goldfish swallowing, the derby ended. As the U.S Public Health Service's chief pathologist said at the time: *"Goldfish have tapeworms. Don't eat them."*

Easy Money

Everyone wants an easy life - and early retirement is a worthy goal. Some lucky souls manage to break free and live a life of leisure. It could be through winning the lottery, selling their ideas of business, or even making shrewd investment decisions.

Then there's Charles Simon - the Frenchman who got paid to literally do nothing.

Simon was a manager of the French railway operator SNCF. Having sat at home for around 12 years, Simon reluctantly gave up the game that he had still been receiving his monthly salary of €5,400 (around $6500). On top of that, the Frenchman also received a €600 annual holiday bonus - and yet it's him that's now suing the company despite having done no work for over a decade.

According to Simon, the situation came about after he uncovered fraudulent practices while working with a contractor to SNCF in 2003. They insisted the top brass give him another role to keep him quiet, and he's been waiting ever since.

He went on to launch a legal claim seeking €500,000 in damages for "loss of career opportunity", which seems a little ungrateful for a full 12 years of fully paid-up holiday time.

This isn't the first time that something like this has happened, either. A hospital worker in Italy managed to fleece his employer for around 15 years after he simply stopped showing up in 2005.

The man reportedly received €538,000 in Salary payments over that time, and it turns out he only did about a week on the job in the first place before pulling the world's longest game of truant.

Supposedly he threatened his original manager to stop her from filing a disciplinary report against him. When she retired, nobody else even knew who he was and so his not-so-elaborate scheme continued.

You could say that he gets his money for nothing, and we're sure his employer would give him a kick for free.

Fragrant Flatulence

Romance brings out strange things in some people. For one inventor, the ever romantic Valentine's Day inspired him to create one of the world's strangest consumable products: scented flatulence pills.

Christian Poincheval had already created an array of scented flatulence pills that had been carefully crafted to make wind smell a little less foul.

As a special addition to the range, he introduced what he described as the "most romantic fart scent of all". With the gentle aroma of ginger and bergamot, a user could supposedly pass wind with aphrodisiac qualities after taking just one pill.

"Say it with love, flavor your farts with ginger", read the advert for the pills which should only be taken once a day - and up to six times a day for those who suffer from excessive flatulence.

The idea for the pills apparently came to Poincheval after a holiday in Switzerland. Having eaten significant quantities of cheese, the man was letting out stenches so vile that his friends held car air fresheners to their noses.

"Everyone needs these pills", he said, "especially me after a curry."

A Cure for Crack

One Frenchman has invented the world's least needed product for one of it's longest standing problems (at least in home improvement circles).

Adrien Herve-Pellissier, a 24-year-old Frenchman from Rennes think's he's cracked the market with his new creation, the "sourire de plombier" or the "plumber's smile".

The product - which is really little more than a very robust pair of underwear - is designed to address the age-old dilemma of the 'builder's bum'. In France it has many other names including the 'Mason's Smile', and so it's clearly a major problem in the country.

Herve-Pellissier recognizes the limitations of his invention, but still thinks it adds real value to the world of construction. Speaking of his work, he commented: "I'm not changing the world... maybe just a bit. It's not like I've found a cure for Aids – just for the builder's crack."

His next move is reportedly to create sweet-smelling underwear for men, so it's clear he's found his niche.

In any case, we can only wish him the best and hope that his product doesn't fall through the cracks.

Are You My Cousin?

Remote and rural parts of the world are often populated by just a handful of families. People come and go, and over time the residents manage to avoid inbreeding (or perhaps they don't). With a population of only around 320,000, Iceland has some serious issues in this regard.

The country is so concerned about accidental inter-familial relations that it's built a mobile app to help people find out whether they are related to a person or not.

The Android mobile app allows users to cross-reference their names against a database to decide whether hooking up with their date is a good idea, or whether they should stop kissing their surprise cousin straight away.

Other quirks of the island nation are also driven by its small population. They even have a phone directory book that lists people by their first names rather than by surnames. The problem is that there are quite literally thousands of Jóns and Gunnars, so it's very hard to get hold of the right people.

At least the Icelanders are no longer communicating in Norse Code!

Rubber Man

Superheroes are generally considered to be strong and resilient, but they always have a weakness. For Superman it was Pink Kryptonite, Johnny Storm struggled with asbestos (who doesn't), and Thor couldn't be without his famed hammer for more than 60 seconds.

As a tech billionaire wearing a suit of armor, Iron Man was relatively free from any of the classic weaknesses - but his likeness in

India can be brought down with just one pin prick.

In 2020, the residents of a small village in Uttar Pradesh were terrified when they spotted what appeared to be Iron Man floating over their houses. He eventually set up shop in a tree and didn't move for days.

The locals thought that the end of times had come, and the few that were familiar with the Marvel protagonist presumably kept quiet or genuinely believed that Tony Stark was real.

The whole fiasco only came to an end when a small bird flew into the tree at some speed - popping Iron Man in the process.

He had been a balloon all along, and it's fair to say you wouldn't want Rubber Man and his powers of floating and popping on your side during a high octane fight.

The Foul-Mouthed Parking Machine

Every good sci-fi enthusiast knows that one day the machines will fight back, but nobody expected it to be a war of words.

One scandal-hit French politician has complained to the powers that be after a parking machine issued 500 tickets that called him a "thieving bastard". Politicians are generally thick skinned and used to insults, but it's not every day that you get insulted by machines.

In this case, Jean-François Copé found that the local parking machines had been printing out extra massages calling him a "total prat" and a "stupid thief".

One employee of the ticketing company (who notably refused to be named) said that it certainly wasn't a member of staff or a hacker, and that the machines just had an aversion to spin doctors and politicians.

Let's face it, it's bad enough paying to park let alone being insulted too. If we're to win this war, we'll clearly need some very strongly worded letters indeed.

Ice Cold Killer

We've all been there - when something needs doing, a little white lie is all that's needed to prompt people into action. For most of us, those little white lies mean overstating the importance of a task, or bringing the deadline forward. For one Ukrainian man, it meant staging a heinous crime.

During a particularly cold winter, one man was fed up with being unable to get his car out of the garage. He did the only logical thing he could think of, and called the police to report an entirely fictitious murder.

Claiming that he had killed his mother's partner by stabbing him, he told the police that the victim "showed no signs of life" but was oddly persistent about the authorities bringing a snow plough with them. He assured them that they would be unable to reach his residence without one, but didn't bank on the police using an all-terrain vehicle to pay him a visit.

Amusingly, as the police pulled up the drive, the man's father-in-law was walking up to the house to bring him some supplies. They had a great relationship, and the man was surprised to be told that he himself had been murdered.

The road was cleared the following morning, but the fake murderer did request that the police come back to widen the track on either side.

He was charged with making a false call, and faced a fine of up to 119 hryvnias (around $4). That's the lightest sentence for homicide ever, even if it was entirely made up!

Puff Puff Pass

Crazy True Tales

Dolphins are considered as one of the smartest species in the animal kingdom, but nobody would have guessed that they had the ability to mimic human stoners and hippies.

Reports from marine biologists suggest that pods of dolphins have been getting high by capturing puffer fish, chewing on the glands containing nerve toxins, and passing them around to their friends.

Dolphins and we humans aren't the only ones with substance abuse issues, though. Horses have been known to seek out the most potent hallucinogenic weeds in fields, while bighorn sheep seem to love narcotic lichens that supposedly cause acid trips.

Most amusing of all are the elephants who get drunk on overripe fruit. They've even been seen leaving certain trees and bushes alone to come back to later when they feel like winding down.

Drink driving is highly dangerous and rightly frowned upon, but can you imagine the terror that a drunken elephant could unleash on our roads?

Looking back at the dolphins, it does seem that we should never have trusted them in the first place. The Hamas political group once arrested one for allegedly being an Israeli 'spy', and the creator was subsequently dubbed Orcapussy, Goldflipper, and Dolphinfidel.

At least he got a better name than the spy koi, James Pond.

Your Drinks Aren't Safe in the Cooler

One night, a thirty-eight-year-old Wisconsin resident by the name of Jeremy Van Ert found himself in a bit of a predicament.

He had been craving a cool alcoholic beverage all day, and decided to treat himself by walking to the local Kwik Trip convenience store to pick up something from their selection.

With nobody behind the counter and no sign of any beers, Van Ert wandered into a much colder section of the store. After a little while spent browsing, he was surprised to find himself locked in.

Van Ert had inadvertently walked into the store's industrial fridge, which automatically locked on the dot of midnight each and every day.

Feeling the cold creep in around him, our unlikely hero made a bold move. Rather than knocking on the door to attract the now present clerk's attention, he opted to hunker down and slam drink after drink until he could no longer feel the cold.

The door unlocked at around 6am the next morning, and a very drunk Van Ert staggered out and got into his truck without paying for any of the booze.

He'd consumed at least 20 bottles, and smashed a whole lot more - so the shop decided that they couldn't let it go.

Van Ert was arrested for felony theft - but also drink driving as he was definitely over the limit.

It's a salutary tale, but one that might be worth thinking about next time you put a bottle in the cooler.

The War That Barely Was

You may know about the Hundred Years' War, and perhaps even know that the Anglo-French wars lasted almost 750 years. Even these days our conflicts drag on for decades despite all the technology available to the world's armies, but even a nuclear skirmish would struggle to compete with possibly the shortest war ever.

We give to you: the 38 minute war!

The Anglo-Zanzibar War was fought between the United Kingdom and the Zanzibar Sultanate in 1896. It was caused by a disagreement regarding who should succeed the dead sultan as ruler of what we now call Tanzania.

During the intense yet very short period of fighting, the usurper of Zanzibar's throne hid away in his palace while the British troops rounded up three cruisers, two gunboats, 150 marines, and 900 soldiers.

The British shot down the Zanzibar flag, and the angry sultan quickly was ousted from his position all in less than hour.

Say what you like about military efficiency, but some people can't even get around to sending an email in an hour, let alone toppling a dictatorship!

Friendly Fire of the Canine Kind

As the Germans advanced on Moscow in 1941, the Soviet troops were put in an almost impossible position. The Germans had a fantastic armored division, and the Soviets didn't have any effective anti-tank weaponry.

Out of desperation, they used highly trained military dogs to destroy their enemies, but things didn't quite go to plan.

Strapping explosives to the dogs, they were released and sent on suicide missions to destroy the enemy equipment.

The German tanks were fitted with machine guns, but they couldn't aim low enough to hit the dogs, and so German infantrymen were left to take potshots at the intrepid Russian hounds with their rifles.

German tank units often stopped in their tracks if they saw battalions of tank destroyer dogs, and the only method they could muster to prevent the Soviet onslaught was the use of flamethrowers.

Unfortunately, bomber dogs were not the perfect tactic that the Russians had expected. They had trained them to crawl under enemy tanks while carrying explosives on their bodies, and were initially coaxed under the war machines with scraps of meat.

The major issue with the plan came down to a technicality. The Soviet dog handlers had trained the canines around Soviet tanks, and they had gotten used to the smell of their diesel engines.

The German tanks, on the other hand, used gasoline. As a result, the confused kamikaze dogs ended up blowing up their allies, and those soldiers who weren't killed surrendered with their dogs.

It's a dog eat dog world out there, but a dog with a bomb can quickly level the playing field no matter what side you're on.

Famous Last Words

Watch what you say, as you never know when your last moments are coming. The wrong words could endure longer than any memory of your best achievements, as the following stories prove.

During the American Civil War, General J. Sedgwick stood up from a bunker and shouted at his troops to do the same. Seeing that they were reluctant, he proclaimed that "they couldn't hit an elephant at this distance", before being shot under the left eye and instantly killed.

Some people, of course, take life a little less seriously. Pope Alexander VI died in 1503, and knowing that he was soon to ascend to the pearly gates, he used his final breath to utter the words "Okay, okay, I'll come. Just give me a moment."

When being read his rights before a death sentence by firing squad, the convicted murderer James W. Rodgers was asked if he had anything left to say. "Bring me a bullet-proof vest" was all he could muster. Suffice to say, he didn't get the vest.

Crazy True Tales

Artists and writers are known for their whimsical ways, both in life and on their deathbeds. The poet Dylan Thomas really did get his poetic justice when he exclaimed "I've had 18 straight whiskeys and I'm alive! I think that must be the record." He promptly died.

Finally, the singer Johnny Ace was once backstage trying to impress some groupies when they expressed concern that he was playing with a gun. "Don't worry, it's not loaded ... see?" he said before blowing his brains out.

Use Protection

A German man once blew himself up while trying to rob a condom machine with a homemade bomb - all on Christmas day.

The 29-year-old and his accomplices attached the bomb to the vending machine before taking cover in the vehicle. Unfortunately, he didn't close his door in time, and was struck in the head by a steel shard (and several condoms) from the resultant explosion.

Although his colleagues made off into the night, the police quickly found them as they were driving a car that was not only covered in the debris from an explosion, but also one that was absolutely full to the brim with (presumably damaged) contraception.

The irony is that the man had previously robbed a hunting store and made off with some very expensive protective clothing.

If he'd used protection whilst robbing the condom machine, he might never have been killed!

Pythagoras' Fear of Flatulence

Pythagoras of Samos is famous for a number of truly impressive feats. For one thing, he was a brilliant mathematician, but also created great works of philosophy and generated political theories that have trickled down through the ages.

For such an impressive man, he died in a very unusual way having been chased to the edge of a bean field.

The story behind his strange demise doesn't help much with making sense of matters, but it all started when Pythagoras founded an Italian school where pupils and initiates were sworn to secrecy. The few reports we have suggest that the men lived a communal and ascetic lifestyle, and were all vegetarian. They were also banned from eating legumes such as beans, because Pythagoras himself took issue with the flatulence-causing fava bean.

It was his aversion to beans that got him in the end, as he was accosted by some unfriendly locals while taking an evening stroll. Having wriggled free from their grip, he ran as fast as he could without stopping to look where he was going.

Before he knew it, the famous mathematician wound up staring down rows upon rows of beans in a field. He refused to enter, and was killed.

Pythagoras could have lived to tell the tale, if only he had bean a little braver.

Mary <u>HAD</u> a Little Lamb

Everyone knows the nursery rhyme "Mary Had a Little Lamb", but few have ever questioned its origins.

You see, Mary really DID have a little lamb. There's no way of corroborating whether it's fleece was white as snow, or whether it followed her to school one day. We can't even really comment on whether that was against the rules, but what's more clear is the fate that befell her poor little lamb.

Young Mary Sawyer, who owned the lamb, sold its wool to raise money for her local church, which was in desperate need of a new and quite expensive roof. She was known to take her lamb with her to market where she sold her wares, but their sweet relationship couldn't last forever.

When a cold and bitter winter hit, Mary's family were pretty strapped for cash (having given all of theirs to the church roof fund) and were forced to butcher the poor lamb for supper.

This is where the song comes from, because while Mary once had a little lamb, she went on to eat it.

Nursery rhymes just aren't the same when you're an adult.

The Cartoon Criminal

In 2007, an unwitting criminal thought that he'd dreamed up the perfect heist. An elderly man living just streets away from his suburban Australian home was known to have a valuable art collection and probably more treasure besides.

The crook devised a plan which entailed sneaking into his target's home while he was sleeping. He had already scoped out the property's two security cameras and carefully disabled them using a can of black spray paint.

Once in the home he would aim to take everything he wanted within five minutes before escaping through a back window into the garden, from where he could leap fences to make it back to his own property.

On the night of his fateful burglary attempt, the young man broke into the house and quickly realized that his target was sleeping. So far, so good. After scouring the ground floor for valuable art, he made his way upstairs and started rummaging around whilst trying to stay quiet.

It was at this stage that his victim woke up and startled him. He pushed through the doorway and ran away, believing that he could never be identified on account of wearing gloves and being so careful with the security cameras.

What he hadn't counted on, however, was the photographic memory of his victim. When coupled with the older gentleman's skills as one of Australia's foremost caricaturists, it made for a pretty accurate e-fit - albeit one with a much larger nose and forehead.

The thief was caught, and his amusing caricature went on display in a local art gallery.

They've since uncovered more of the man's crimes, but the details are still sketchy.

The Bungling Broadcast Corporation

The British Broadcasting Corporation (BBC) is known for the impartial and high quality programming it provides. It's television and radio broadcasts are known throughout the world, and are often tipped as a go-to source of expert opinion in matters of politics, business, science, and global events.

It goes without saying that many people rely on the BBC for knowledge and news, but the corporation's guestlist hasn't always been populated by the great and the good of journalism and analysis.

In one fateful incident, producers had booked the editor of a technology news website to discuss a court case involving Apple. Guy Kewney was due on air at precisely 09:30am, and so had arrived 25 minutes earlier in preparation for his slot on the business news show. On checking in, he was met by confused looks from receptionists. To their mind, Guy Kewney was already speaking to the cameras in studio 2 after having turned up with an hour to spare.

Unbeknownst to the BBC crew members, the interviewer was discussing the technicalities of the Apple court battle with Guy Goma - a graduate from the Congo who had been wrongly booked into the studio as his technology expert namesake. Goma had arrived so early because he had actually been scheduled to have a job interview and wanted to make a good impression.

Mr Goma was asked three questions live on air, each time responding that he was "very surprised". The business presenter managed to pass a message to the show's editor that her guest seemed "very breathless and nervous". It was only then that they realized the real interviewee was waiting in reception, and that they'd asked a very flustered graduate to give his opinions to a watching TV audience of at least a million people.

The feed was pulled from the air and the real Guy Kewney had his interview later that day.

Mr Goma, on the other hand, felt that his interview had been "very short" but reassured the producers that he could return and was "happy to speak about any situation".

It's safe to say that he wasn't hired, but the producers did at least think that he was a stand up guy.

Barter Days Are Ahead

Crazy True Tales

It's hard to get onto the property market. The housing market is dominated by large corporations and wealthy landlords, making it ever harder for young people (or anyone for that matter) to buy a home of their own.

Not everyone is willing to settle for a life of renting, however. On at least two occasions, determined bargainers have exchanged their way up from next to nothing all the way to a full blown property.

The original trading prodigy was a 26-year-old man from Montreal. Kyle MacDonald started with a single red paperclip, which traded for a pen that looked like a fish.

MacDonald then went on to trade the aquatic-themed pen for a handmade doorknob. This time he traded that for a camping stove, which was quickly exchanged for a 100-watt generator.

The next trade was for an 'instant party kit', which comprised of an empty keg and a neon Budweiser beer sign. This naturally was snapped up by a radio host for the princely sum of one snowmobile.

Eventually, the snowmobile found a new home with somebody who was willing to give up an afternoon with Alice Cooper, which was traded for a KISS snow globe and eventually a paid role in the film *Donna on Demand*.

It just so happened that Corbin Bernsen was the director of the aforementioned movie. As a prolific collector of snowglobes, he was quite happy to give up a cameo role in the production, which was traded to the town with several wannabe actors for a two bedroom farmhouse.

Inspired by MacDonald's entrepreneurial spirit, Californian Demi Skipper tried her hand at the challenge starting with just a bobby pin. After six months and 25 trades, she eventually executed her final swap from a 2011 Jeep to a luxurious wooden cabin.

It may seem like a hard ask, but the moral of the story is clear: next time the bank turns you down for a loan, just ask for a paperclip.

Holiday from Hell

Travelling rarely goes exactly to plan, but that's part of what makes it so interesting. Sadly for one couple, their honeymoon travels were less 'interesting' and more 'plain disastrous'.

Stefan and Erika Svanström married in Stockholm, Sweden before setting out on what should have been the trip of a lifetime. They had only made it to Munich in Germany when they were stranded by a heavy snowstorm. Once the weather had cleared, they made their way to Cairns, Australia where they were greeted by a cyclone.

In a bid to avoid the rising floodwaters, they left for Perth - where raging brushfires had taken hold, sending billowing plumes of smoke into the sky. This prompted the Svanströms to head on to Christchurch in New Zealand, just hours before a major earthquake.

Not content with the trouble they'd seen so far, they travelled to Tokyo, Japan only to be at the heart of an earthquake and tsunami. Happily, the final leg of their trip took the form of a thoroughly uneventful week in China.

Their marriage survived, but we can't help but wonder if they should be banned from travelling in the future.

Final Words

That may be the end of our almanac of jovial real-life stories, but the world is still turning and more people are embarrassing themselves each and every day.

Our hope is that this comedic collection has lifted your spirits and helped you to see the brighter side of life. Our planet is a remarkable and strange place, with wonder around each and every corner. It's all the same whether you're actively looking for it or finding it conveniently compiled across the pages of this book.

When you're laughing, everything is right with the world. As Mark Twain put it, *"against the assault of laughter, nothing can stand"*.

Author's note

Thank you for reading my book. I very much hope you enjoyed it and found it amusing. You may be aware that Amazon reviews are critical for independent authors; without these, my work will never be seen, that is just the way the system works. I would like to ask you to spend two minutes to leave a review for me, and be assured I personally read all my reviews. Your review will have a massive social influence on who will read my book as most people check the reviews. If you have never left a review before, just give one or two points around your main impressions and what you enjoyed. Thanks, please click on the LINK below or scan QR code:

[Help Adam by leaving a review](#)

Printed in Great Britain
by Amazon